Introduction

The two Corrective Reading Mastery Tests for Decoding B1: *Decoding Strategies* assess individual student achievement in terms of specific learning objectives. This Examiner's Manual explains the procedures of administering and grading the tests. Test 1 is a mid-program test to be administered when the students have completed the first thirty-five lessons of the B1 program. Test 2 covers the skills taught in the second part of the B1 program and is administered when students have completed Lessons 36–65.

The mastery tests serve two major purposes. First of all, they provide documentation of a student's performance after she or he has completed certain parts of the program. They serve as posttests, and they are carefully designed for this purpose. (Do not use the Corrective Reading Placement Test as a posttest measure. It is not designed to evaluate progress, only to place students.)

Secondly, the mastery tests are a criterion-referenced measure that samples all decoding objectives in the program—something that is not done on the individual reading checkouts. Student performance on the tests indicates the extent to which the objectives have been mastered.

These mastery tests are not designed to serve as an ongoing measurement tool. They are not detailed enough in the different skills taught in the program. Instead, the individual reading checkouts provide an ongoing test of decoding proficiency. The word-attack skills: individual tests and the inprogram mastery tests also provide a standard by which to evaluate the group. However, the information provided by the checkouts should serve as the *primary guide* for the teacher to evaluate individual students: to identify problems, to determine the rate at which the program material is presented, and to judge a student ready for the next level of the program.

In short, the Corrective Reading decoding programs provide good information about the day-to-day performance of individual students. However, it is important that this information be used along with the results of these mid- and end-of-program mastery tests to thoroughly assess each student's performance.

The Decoding B1 Tests 1 and 2 include both a group and individual section. The first section of each test is administered to the group. While students are completing their worksheets, the examiner administers the individual section to each student. For the individual section, the examiner exchanges test booklets with the student and marks incorrect responses as the test is being given in the student's test booklet.

To ensure accurate measurement of your students' progress, conduct the test sessions in a manner that inspires the students' confidence and minimizes anxiety. Some preparation on your part is important for each test session to run smoothly.

Administering the Tests

SCHEDULING

If possible, schedule testing of students within a week after they have completed either the first or the second part of the program. You may want to test two or three students a day so your regular classroom schedule is not disrupted. You can expect most students to complete each test in ten to fifteen minutes.

Test 1 should be administered to the students after they have completed Lesson 35 of the Decoding B1 program. This test is not appropriate for those students who place at Lesson 1 in the Decoding B2 program and begin the program there. Test 2 should be given after the students have completed the Decoding B1 program—Lessons 36–65.

PREPARING FOR THE TESTS

Before giving any of the tests, familiarize yourself with this Examiner's Manual and the test booklet for Tests 1 and 2, each of which includes a Student Profile at the beginning of each test, a Group Section, and an Individual Section.

Have the students write their names on the cover of their test booklet. The Student Profiles must have the student's and the teacher's name on it. You may want to write these in before administering the test.

MATERIALS

For the Group Sections of the tests, each student will need a copy of the test booklet and a pencil with an eraser. Be sure to have extra pencils on hand.

To administer the Individual Sections, you will need the student's copy of the appropriate test; an extra, clean copy of the test for the student to read; this Examiner's Manual; a stopwatch; and a clipboard. The student will read from the clean copy of the test while you mark the errors on the student's copy. There should be no marks on the clean copy.

TESTING ENVIRONMENT

For the group sections of the Decoding B1 Mastery Tests, each student must have a desk or table space large enough for the test booklet. To discourage copying, place the students as far apart as possible.

The individual sections of the tests should be administered in a quiet place, preferably away from all other students.

Neither Test 1 nor Test 2 has strict time limits, and the students should be encouraged to take the time they need to read accurately. It may be necessary to encourage some students frequently.

SCORING PROCEDURES

- Word-identification items should be scored by recording the incorrect response above the misidentified word in the student's test booklet. Recording incorrect responses is recommended for diagnostic purposes.
- If the student doesn't respond to a word within ten seconds, omits a word, or says, "I don't know that word," slash the word to indicate an error.
- If the student self-corrects the initial error, write SC next to the incorrect response. Allow the student five self-corrects. Count the remaining self-corrects as errors.
- If the student vacillates between two responses, ask, "What is it?" and record the final response.

After marking the student's word-identification errors for each test part, count the number and enter the total on the line that follows each test part.

- For scoring comprehension questions, see the answer key for Test 1 on page 3 and for Test 2 on page 5.

RESPONDING TO THE STUDENT

From time to time during the test, praise the student for working hard, even if her or his performance is poor. After each part, briefly acknowledge that the task has been completed. Say, "That was fine," or the like. Do not tell a student that he or she did well following an incorrect response.

Decoding B1: Mastery Test 1

(After Lesson 35)
(Pass out the test booklets. Tell the students to write their names on the cover of the booklet.)

THE GROUP SECTION

Today I would like you to do some workbook activities, read some words, and read a story to show how much you have learned about reading.

Part 1   Writing letters for sounds
1. **Open your test booklet to page 2.**
   Write your name at the top of the worksheet.
   (Wait.)

Ready? Everybody, touch part 1. ✔
2. **You're going to write the letter or letters for each sound that I say. You know three ways to write the sound k. Write them in the first three blanks. ✔**
3. **Next sound: ŏŏŏ. What sound? ŏŏŏ. Write it.**
4. (Repeat step 2 for **shshsh, ōōōll, ch, ing, ththth, ĭĭĭ.**)

Part 2   Writing words without endings
1. **Find part 2. ✔**
   The words in the first column have endings.
2. **Touch the first word. ✔ What word?** *Raked.*
3. **Next word. ✔ What word?** *Dropping.*
4. (Repeat step 3 for **nearly, shortest, grinned.**)
5. **Later you'll write the same words without endings in the second column.**

Parts 3-4   Matching completion/Sentence copying
   Complete parts 3 and 4 on your own.
   I will call on each of you to read for me.

ANSWER KEY—GROUP SECTION

1. (Any order: k, c, ck), o, sh, ol, ch, ing, th, i

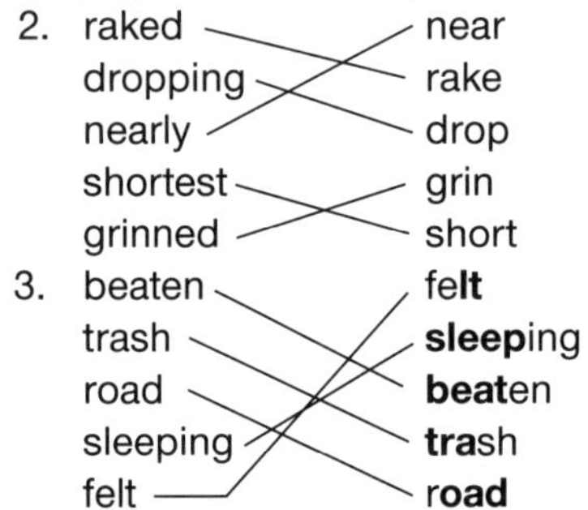

4. The tramp gets in shape.

At this time, administer the Individual Section of the test to each student.

THE INDIVIDUAL SECTION

As soon as the student is comfortably seated, place his or her test booklet on the clipboard. Make sure that errors can be recorded unobtrusively. Fill in the identification information if you have not already done so. Once the desired rapport has been established, give the student a clean copy of the appropriate test booklet.

Parts 5-9   Word reading
1. (Point to part 5 and say:)
   Now I would like you to read some words. Read all the words in each part. Read across as you do in your Student Book. Read as carefully as you can.
2. (Mark the errors as the student reads. Remember to record incorrect responses. Repeat for parts 6, 7, 8, and 9.)

Parts 10 and 11   Story reading

1. (Direct the student to the story and say:)
   Before you read this story to me, I am going to give you two minutes to study it. Ask me about any words you don't know.

2. (Give the student up to two minutes to study the story. Answer any questions about vocabulary. After two minutes or when the student is ready, say:)
   You're going to read this story to me as quickly and carefully as you can. Then I'll ask some questions about what happened in the story.

3. (Tell the student to begin and start timing the reading.)

   (Count any sounding out as an error. Allow five self-corrections. Count any subsequent self-corrections as errors. Mark errors in the student's test booklet as the student reads. If there are any interruptions, have the student start again.)

   (When the student has finished reading, record the time and the total number of errors on the lines provided at the bottom of the story.)

Part 12   Oral comprehension questions
   I'll ask some questions. If you don't know the answer to a question, you may look back in the story, but you have to find the answer quickly.

(Record the answers in the student's test booklet. Allow the student thirty seconds to respond to each question.)
   1. **When did the tramp go to bed?**
   2. **Name 2 things the tramp did for work at the ranch.**
   3. **How long did the tramp stay at the ranch?**
   4. **What did the tramp tell the rancher he needed?**
   5. **Did the tramp get more to eat?**

ANSWER KEY FOR PART 12
ORAL COMPREHENSION QUESTIONS

1. When the sun was dropping in the west. (Accept reasonable responses, such as, When the sun went down in the west.)
2. He sheared sheep. He made gates and pens for pigs. He dug holes for trees. (Accept any 2 responses.)
3. Ten weeks
4. More meat and beans
5. Yes

Write an **X** next to the answers that are wrong and enter the total number of errors in the blank.

After administering the Individual Section, remind the student to complete the worksheet if she or he has not already done so.

This completes the individually administered section of the Decoding B1 Mastery Test 1. Repeat parts 5-12 with each student.

RECORDING TEST 1 RESULTS

After administering the entire test and completing the scoring, enter the student's test results on his or her Student Profile, which appears at the beginning of Test 1. Objectives matching each test item appear on page 6.

For each part, enter the number of errors in the Number of Errors column across from the appropriate part number. For example, if a student made one error in part 1, record a 1 in the Number of Errors column across from part 1. Next, determine whether the student passed or failed the part by comparing the number of errors with the criterion for passing. In this case, record a + in the Pass-Fail column.

GROUP SUMMARY

After completing the Student Profile of each student in the group, summarize the performance of the group, using the Group Summary Form for Test 1 on page 7. In order to assess the progress of the group, record the following information on the Group Summary Form: the student's name and a + or 0 indicating whether the student passed or failed the skill labeled at the top of the column. Then fill in the column labeled, "Percentage of Skills Passed by Student" and "Percentage of Students Mastering Each Skill."

To find the percentage passed for each student, use table 1 on page 9. Count the number of skills mastered and look below that number to find the percentage passed by the student.

Use table 3 to determine the percentage of students mastering each skill. First locate the total number of students in the group in the first column on the left; then determine the number of students who mastered each skill, and locate this number along the bottom. The point of intersection of the two rows gives the percentage of students who mastered the skill. Enter these percentages along the bottom row of the Group Summary Form.

DIAGNOSIS AND REMEDIATION

Students are expected to pass the major skill areas of the Decoding B1 Mastery Test 1 with approximately 90 percent accuracy. If a student's overall performance, as indicated in the column next to her or his name on the Group Summary Form, is below 85 to 90 percent, it is recommended that the student be reviewed on deficit skill areas before advancing in the Decoding B1 program.

If the entire group is weak in a skill area, as indicated by a percentage below 80 to 85 on the bottom row of the summary form, then all the students should be taken through the review lessons specified for that skill area on the Student Profile.

After reviewing deficit skill areas with individual students or with the group, readminister those parts of the mastery test that the students failed previously. You may want to use the student's original booklet, scoring in a different color, in order to compare responses.

If a student fails a skill area, a prescription is provided in the far right column of the Student Profile. The prescriptions suggested are groups of lessons taken from the Decoding B1 program. The student should not be reviewed on just the skills failed on the mastery test. Rather, it is suggested that entire lessons be presented so the students receive well-balanced instruction without excessive drill on specific skill weaknesses. You may still wish to concentrate instructional time on the deficit skill areas, but it is recommended as a minimum that the student read the worksheet words and story for each review lesson. For example, if a student is weak on **ed, ly, er,** or **ing** endings, part 8, you would present Lessons 23, 26, and 28-35.

When the students fail to meet the rate and/or accuracy criteria for the story reading, it is important that they practice reading the stories in Lessons 28-35. They should practice story reading daily until they can read these familiar passages fluently. It is often helpful to have the student read the story silently before reading out loud. Have students practice segments of one hundred words until they can read several passages in a story at a minimum rate of 75 words per minute—or 100 words in 1 minute and 20 seconds—with no more than 2 errors. If students do not reach these criteria, they will have trouble succeeding in the remainder of the Decoding B1 lessons because of inadequate fluency.

Students who fail the comprehension section, part 12, should be reviewed on the same lessons as those who do not meet the rate-accuracy criteria, parts 10 and 11. These students should be asked all the comprehension questions specified in the remediation lesson and any additional questions the teacher may add to make sure that the student has understood the story. It is also recommended that the students retell each story after they have read it.

Decoding B1: Mastery Test 2

(After Lesson 65)
(Pass out the test booklets.
Make sure each student gets the correct booklet.)

THE GROUP SECTION

Today I would like you to do some workbook activities, read some words, and read a story to show how much you have learned about reading.

Part 1   Identifying letter combinations
   1. **Open your test booklet to page 6.**
   Write your name at the top of the worksheet.
   (Wait.)
   Ready? Everybody, touch part 1. ✔
   Later you're going to cross out the words that don't have W–H in them.

Part 2   Writing words without endings
   1. **Find part 2. ✔**
   The words in the first column have endings.
   2. **Touch the first word. ✔ What word?** *Firing.*
   3. **Next word. ✔ What word?** *Closer.*
   4. (Repeat step 3 for **zipped, hotter.**)
   5. **Later you'll write the same words without endings in the second column.**

*Parts 3-4   Following instructions/Writing
         compound words*
   Complete parts 3 and 4 on your own. I will call on each of you to read for me.

ANSWER KEY—GROUP SECTION

   1. where ~~with~~ ~~that~~ when ~~how~~ wheel
      ~~word~~ ~~then~~ what why ~~week~~ who
   2. firing — hot
      closer — close
      zipped — fire
      hotter — zip
   3. louder, <u>first</u>
   4. maybe, anybody, nearly, herself

At this time, administer the Individual Section of the test to each student.

THE INDIVIDUAL SECTION

As soon as the student is comfortably seated, place his or her test booklet on the clipboard. Make sure that errors can be recorded unobtrusively. Fill in the identification information if you have not already done so. Once the desired rapport has been established, give the student a clean copy of the appropriate test booklet.

Parts 5-10   Word reading
   1. (Point to part 5 and say:)
   Now I would like you to read some words. Read all the words in each part. Read across as you do in your Student Book. Read as carefully as you can.
   2. (Mark the errors as the student reads. Remember to record incorrect responses. Repeat for parts 6, 7, 8, 9, and 10.)

Parts 11 and 12   Story reading
   1. (Direct the student to the story and say:)
   Before you read this story to me, I am going to

give you two minutes to study it. Ask me about any words you don't know.

2. (Give the student up to two minutes to study the story. Answer any questions about vocabulary. After two minutes or when the student is ready, say:) **You're going to read this story to me as quickly and carefully as you can. Then I'll ask some questions about what happened in the story.**

3. (Tell the student to begin and start *timing* the reading.)

   (Count any sounding out as an error. Allow five self-corrections. Count subsequent self-corrections as errors. Mark errors in the student's test booklet as the student reads. If there are any interruptions, have the student start again.)

   (When the student has finished reading, record the time and the total number of errors on the lines provided at the bottom of the story.)

Part 13   Oral comprehension questions
   I'll ask some questions. If you don't know the answer to a question, you may look back in the story, but you have to find the answer quickly.

(Record the answers in the student's test booklet. Allow the student thirty seconds to respond to each question.)
   1. **Why did the ship begin to sink?**
   2. **Why did the people not sink?**
   3. **What did the one man whisper?**
   4. **How did the people help him?**
   5. **Where did they go in the boat?**

ANSWER KEY FOR PART 13
ORAL COMPREHENSION QUESTIONS

   1. A bolt came out of the ship. (Accept reasonable responses, such as, Something that was holding the boat together fell off.)
   2. They were holding on to boards.
   3. "I can't swim."
   4. The people grabbed on to him and kept him from sinking. (Accept other reasonable responses.)
   5. They went to shore.

Write an **X** next to the answers that are wrong and enter the total number of errors in the blank.

After administering the Individual Section, remind the student to complete the worksheet if he or she has not already done so.

This completes the individually administered section of the Decoding B1 Mastery Test 2. Repeat parts 5-13 with each student.

RECORDING TEST 2 RESULTS

After administering the entire test and completing the scoring, enter the student's test results on his or her Student Profile, which appears at the beginning of Test 2. Objectives matching each test item appear on page 6. Follow the same procedure as for Test 1.

GROUP SUMMARY

Follow the same procedure as for Test 1, but be sure to use the Group Summary Form for Test 2, which appears on page 7, and the tables that appear on the back cover.

DIAGNOSIS AND REMEDIATION

Follow the diagnosis and remediation guidelines as for Test 1, which appear on page 4 of this Examiner's Manual.

Students who fail to meet the rate and accuracy criteria for Test 2 should practice rereading the specified Decoding B1 stories until they are reading familiar content at a rate of 90 words per minute. It is recommended that students practice segments of one hundred words in stories 45, 46, 60–65 until they can read several segments at 90 words per minute, that is, 100 words in 1 minute and 6 seconds, with no more than 2 errors. It is critical that a student's fluency is improved before he or she proceeds to the Decoding B2 program.

MASTERY OBJECTIVES

Following are the mastery objectives for Decoding B1: *Decoding Strategies,* Test 1 and Test 2. Each part of the mastery tests has been designed to test a particular skill area which can be found on the objectives chart. The first column lists the skill area, the middle column specifies in detail the student behavior required, and the last column lists the test numbers in which the skill is tested.

Skill	Mastery Objective	Test

WORD IDENTIFICATION

Skill	Mastery Objective	Test
Writing Letters for Sounds	Upon hearing sounds, the student will write the letters that make the sounds.	1
Identifying Letter Combinations	The student will identify letter combinations within words.	2
Writing Words Without Endings	After reading words with endings, the student will write the words without endings.	1, 2
Matching Completion	The student will make two words match by adding letters to the incomplete words.	1
Following Instructions	The student will follow a set of written instructions.	2
Sentence Copying	The student will copy a sentence accurately.	1
Writing Compound Words	The student will write compound words.	2
Short-Vowel Words	Given phonetically regular monosyllabic words containing the short-vowel sound **a, e, i, o,** or **u,** the student will identify the words.	1, 2
Long-Vowel Words	Given phonetically regular monosyllabic long-vowel words containing either a silent **e** at the end or a medial double **ee,** the student will identify the word.	1
Consonant Digraphs	Given a word containing the consonant digraph **sh, th, wh,** or **ch,** the student will identify the word.	2
Sound Combinations **ea, ar, ai, ol, or, oa, ou, ow, ch**	Given a word containing a sound combination, the student will identify the word.	1, 2
Word Endings **ed, ly, er, s, ing, est, ery**	Given a word containing word endings, the student will identify the word.	1, 2
ed Endings in Short-Vowel Words	Given a phonetically regular short-vowel word with any one of three **ed** endings, the student will identify the word.	2
Irregular Words	Given phonetically irregular words from Lessons 1–65, the student will identify the words.	1, 2

STORY READING

Skill	Mastery Objective	Test
Rate and Accuracy	Given a narrative passage containing familiar vocabulary and characters but unfamiliar story content, the student will read the passage at a minimum rate with approximately 96-97% accuracy or above. (See chart below)	1, 2
Comprehension	Orally given literal comprehension questions, the student will answer the questions at 75% accuracy or above.	1, 2

Test	Story Length	WPM	Time Limit	Error Limit
1	100 words	75	80 secs. (1 min. 20 secs.)	4
2	121 words	90	90 secs. (1 min. 30 secs.)	4

Test 1
GROUP SUMMARY FORM

CORRECTIVE READING MASTERY TESTS **DECODING B1: Decoding Strategies**

Teacher _______________________ **Group** _______________________ **Date** _______________________

Student	Percentage of Skills Passed by Student	Group Section				Individual Section							
		1	2	3	4	5	6	7	8	9	10	11	12
Percentage of Students Mastering Each Skill													

Test 2
GROUP SUMMARY FORM

CORRECTIVE READING MASTERY TESTS

DECODING B1: Decoding Strategies

Teacher ___________________   **Group** ___________________   **Date** ___________________

Student	Percentage of Skills Passed by Student	Group Section				Individual Section								
		1	2	3	4	5	6	7	8	9	10	11	12	13
Percentage of Students Mastering Each Skill														

PERCENTAGE OF SKILLS PASSED BY STUDENT

TABLE 1 (for Test 1)

Number of Skills Mastered	1	2	3	4	5	6	7	8	9	10	11	12
Percentage Passed	8	17	25	33	42	50	58	67	75	83	92	100

TABLE 2 (for Test 2)

Number of Skills Mastered	1	2	3	4	5	6	7	8	9	10	11	12	13
Percentage Passed	8	15	23	31	38	46	54	61	69	77	85	92	100

PERCENTAGE OF STUDENTS MASTERING EACH SKILL

TABLE 3 (for Tests 1 and 2)

Number of Students in Group

	1	2	3	4	5	6	7	8	9	10	11	12	13	14	15	16	17	18	19	20
1	100																			
2	50	100																		
3	33	67	100																	
4	25	50	75	100																
5	20	40	60	80	100															
6	17	33	50	67	83	100														
7	14	29	43	57	71	86	100													
8	13	25	38	50	63	75	88	100												
9	11	22	33	44	55	67	78	89	100											
10	10	20	30	40	50	60	70	80	90	100										
11	9	18	27	36	45	55	64	73	82	91	100									
12	8	17	25	33	42	50	58	67	75	83	92	100								
13	8	15	23	31	38	46	54	62	69	77	85	92	100							
14	7	14	22	29	36	43	50	57	64	71	79	86	93	100						
15	7	13	20	27	33	40	47	53	60	67	73	80	87	93	100					
16	6	13	19	25	31	38	44	50	56	63	69	75	81	88	94	100				
17	6	13	18	24	29	35	41	47	53	59	65	71	76	82	88	94	100			
18	6	11	17	22	28	33	39	44	50	55	61	67	72	77	83	88	94	100		
19	5	11	16	21	26	32	37	42	47	53	58	63	68	74	79	84	89	95	100	
20	5	10	15	20	25	30	35	40	45	50	55	60	65	70	75	80	85	90	95	100

Number of Students Who Mastered the Skill

Decoding B1
Mastery Test Examiner's Manual

R74782.02

SRA
McGraw-Hill

A Division of The McGraw·Hill Companies

Decoding Strategies

**Mastery Test Booklet
Decoding B1**

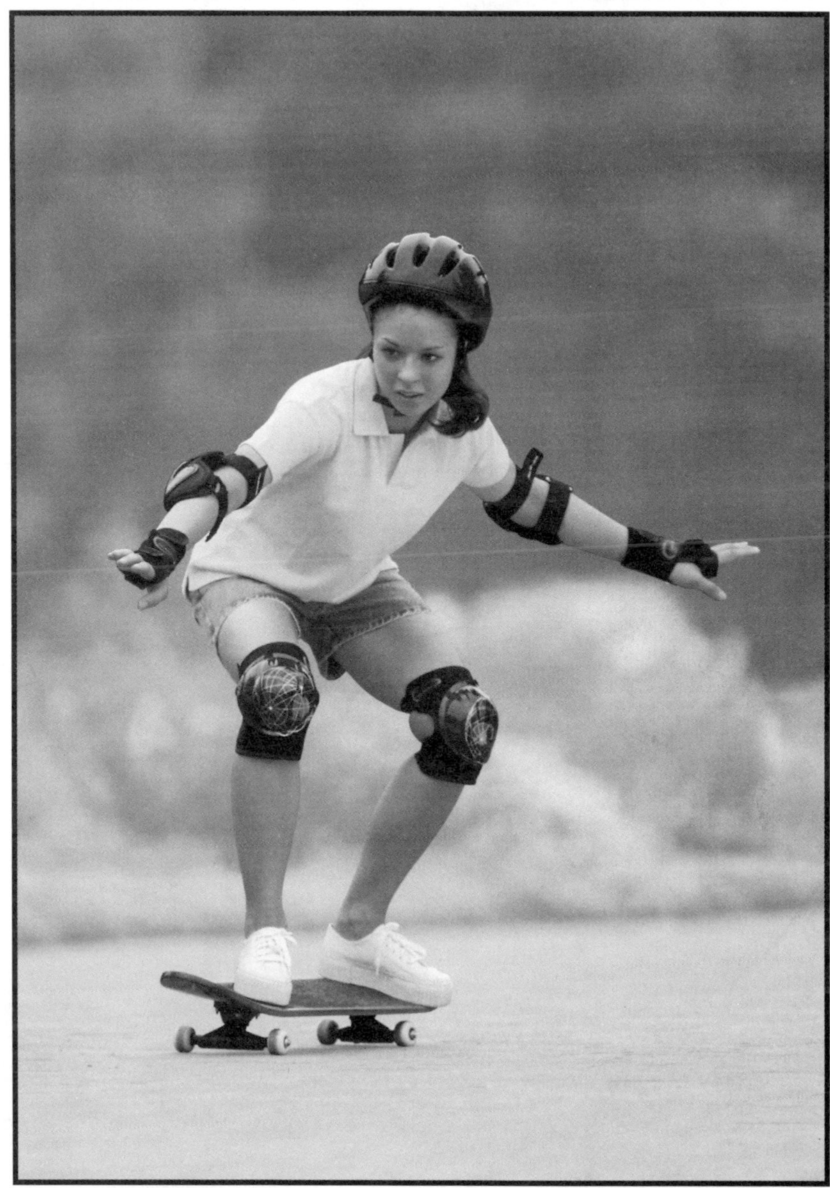

PHOTO CREDITS
Cover Photo: KS Studios

A Division of The McGraw·Hill Companies

2002 Imprint
Copyright © 1999 by SRA/McGraw-Hill.

All rights reserved. Except as permitted under the United States Copyright Act, no part of this publication may be reproduced or distributed in any form or by any means, or stored in a database or retrieval system, without the prior written permission of the publisher, unless otherwise indicated.

Send all inquiries to:
SRA/McGraw-Hill
8787 Orion Place
Columbus, Ohio 43240-4027

Printed in the United States of America.

R74782.01

13 14   MAZ 07 06 05 04

DECODING B1 MASTERY TEST 1
STUDENT PROFILE

Student _______________________ **Teacher** _______________________ **Date** _______________

<table>
<tr><th colspan="2">Skills tested</th><th>Number
of errors</th><th>Pass
criterion</th><th>Pass +
Fail 0</th><th>If failed, review
these lessons.</th></tr>
<tr><td rowspan="4">GROUP SECTION</td><td colspan="5">WORD IDENTIFICATION</td></tr>
<tr><td>1 Writing Letters for Sounds</td><td></td><td>Pass if
0–1 error</td><td></td><td>27–30</td></tr>
<tr><td>2 Writing Words without Endings</td><td></td><td>Pass if
0 errors</td><td></td><td>23, 25, 27, 29</td></tr>
<tr><td>3 Matching Completion</td><td></td><td>Pass if
0 errors</td><td></td><td>1–4</td></tr>
<tr><td>4 Sentence Copying</td><td></td><td>Pass if
0 errors</td><td></td><td>1–3</td></tr>
<tr><td rowspan="9">INDIVIDUAL SECTION</td><td>5 Short-Vowel Words</td><td></td><td>Pass if
0–1 error</td><td></td><td>1–9, 15, 16, 20, 25</td></tr>
<tr><td>6 Long-Vowel Words</td><td></td><td>Pass if
0–1 error</td><td></td><td>6, 8–10, 24–26</td></tr>
<tr><td>7 Sound Combinations</td><td></td><td>Pass if
0–1 error</td><td></td><td>1–9, 34, 35</td></tr>
<tr><td>8 Word Endings ed, ly, er</td><td></td><td>Pass if
0–1 error</td><td></td><td>23, 26, 28–35</td></tr>
<tr><td>9 Irregular Words</td><td></td><td>Pass if
0–1 error</td><td></td><td>27, 29–31</td></tr>
<tr><td colspan="5">STORY READING   Time</td></tr>
<tr><td>10 Rate (Time)</td><td></td><td>Pass if 80
secs. or less</td><td></td><td>28–35</td></tr>
<tr><td>11 Accuracy (Errors)</td><td></td><td>Pass if
0–4 errors</td><td></td><td>28–35</td></tr>
<tr><td>12 Comprehension</td><td></td><td>Pass if
0–1 error</td><td></td><td>28–35</td></tr>
</table>

STUDENT PROFILE TEST 1 1

TEST 1

1

_____________ _____________ _____________ _____________

_____________ _____________ _____________ _____________

2 The words in the first column have endings.
Write the same words without endings in the second column.

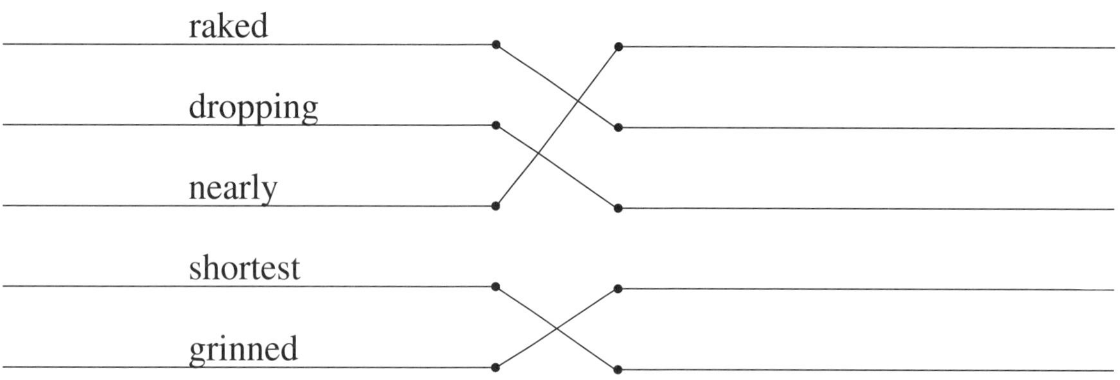

raked

dropping

nearly

shortest

grinned

3 Match the words and complete them.

beaten   fe

trash   ing

road   en

sleeping   sh

felt   r

4  Copy this sentence:
The tramp gets in shape.

____

Individual Section

5   pack   fell   ramp   win   dug
    not   get   bum   pit   drop

5   Errors ______

6   gate   hope   time   week   rider
    nose   fake   wheel   like   shape

6   Errors ______

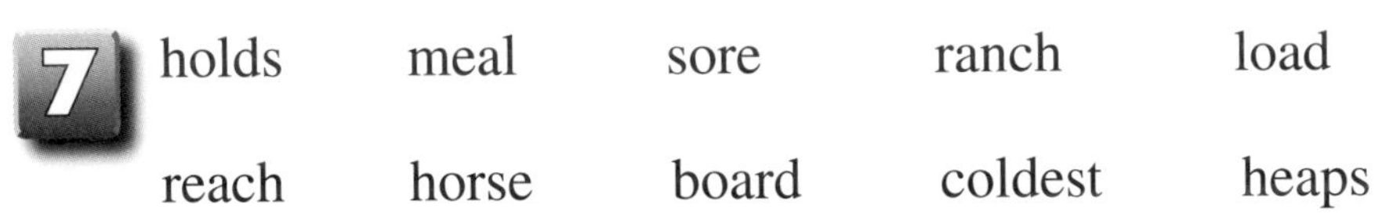

7   holds   meal   sore   ranch   load
    reach   horse   board   coldest   heaps

7   Errors ______

8   sweeping   hammer   yearly   grinned   likely
    stayed   mopping   handed   popper   bigger

8   Errors ______

9   minutes   any   people   couldn't   money

9   Errors ______

The tramp was getting in shape. When he got up, the sun was coming up over the hill in the east. When he went to bed, the sun was dropping in the west. He worked and worked every day. He sheared sheep. He made gates and pens for pigs. He dug holes for trees. He was getting thinner and thinner.

The tramp had stayed at the ranch for ten weeks. He told the rancher, "I need more meat and beans." "Yes," she said. "You have worked and worked. You are faster and thinner. You may have more meat and beans.

10 Time ___________   **11** Errors ______

12

Record student's answers here:

1. When did the tramp go to bed?

____

2. Name 2 things the tramp did for work at the ranch.

____

3. How long did the tramp stay at the ranch?

____

4. What did the tramp tell the rancher he needed?

____

5. Did the tramp get more to eat?

____

12 Errors ______

Student ______________________________ Teacher ______________________________ Date ______________

	Skills tested		Number of errors	Pass criterion	Pass + Fail 0	If failed, review these lessons.
GROUP SECTION	**WORD IDENTIFICATION**					
	1 Identifying Letter Combinations			Pass if 0–1 error		40, 44, 45
	2 Writing Words without Endings			Pass if 0–1 error		52, 58–60
	3 Following Instructions			Pass if 0 errors		46, 47, 56
INDIVIDUAL SECTION	**4** Writing Compound Words			Pass if 0 errors		37–40, 42–45, 48, 62
	5 Short-Vowel Words			Pass if 0–1 error		49, 51–53, 59
	6 Consonant Digraphs			Pass if 0–1 error		9, 12, 47, 48, 52
	7 *ed* Endings in Short-Vowel Words			Pass if 0–1 error		13, 49, 58–61
	8 Word Endings *s, ing, est, er,* and *ery*			Pass if 0–1 error		27, 31, 45, 49, 63, 64
	9 Sound Combinations *ai, oa, or, ol, ea, ou, ow*			Pass if 0–2 errors		51, 52, 55, 61, 62
	10 Irregular Words			Pass if 0–1 error		50, 57–63
	STORY READING	**Time**				
	11 Rate (Time)			Pass if 80 secs. or less		61–65
	12 Accuracy (Errors)			Pass if 0–4 errors		61–65
	13 Comprehension			Pass if 0–1 error		61–65

TEST 2

 **1** Cross out the words that don't have **wh.**

where	with	that	when	how	wheel
word	then	what	why	week	who

 **2** The words in the first column have endings.
Write the same words without endings in the second column.

firing

closer

zipped

hotter

3 Write the word **louder.** Make a line over **loud.** ___________________

Write the word **first.** Make a line under **ir.** ___________________

4 Write the words.

____may____	+	____be____	=	___________________
____any____	+	____body____	=	___________________
____near____	+	____ly____	=	___________________
____her____	+	____self____	=	___________________

Individual Section

5 plop list gum dress tramp

stand crest pond fix must

5 Errors ______

6 smash when chips shop things

whisper there fresh wheels brush

6 Errors ______

7 dressed pinned spotted happened handed

dragged lifted zipped stepped slammed

7 Errors ______

8 trying plants bragging feels slaps

fastest slippery campers slowest teller

8 Errors ______

9 main please boards form bolt

painted beat grow older croak

could loud should mouth ouch

9 Errors ______

11

People were going in a ship from one land to another. They were sailing the sea when a bolt came out of the ship. And the ship began to sink. Men, women, and dogs were in the water. People were swimming and shouting. But the people and dogs were not sinking. They were holding on to boards. They yelled and yelled. One man did not yell. He whispered. This is what that man said, "I can't swim."

The other people grabbed on to him and kept him from sinking. Then a boat came by. A few people dragged him to the boat. When everybody was in the boat, they went to shore. They went faster and faster. They were saved.

11 Time ____________   **12** Errors _______

13 *Record student's answers here:*

1. Why did the ship begin to sink?

____

2. Why did the people not sink?

____

3. What did the one man whisper? _______________________________

4. How did the people help him?

____

5. Where did they go in the boat? _______________________________

13 Errors _______

Decoding Strategies

Mastery Test Booklet
Decoding B1

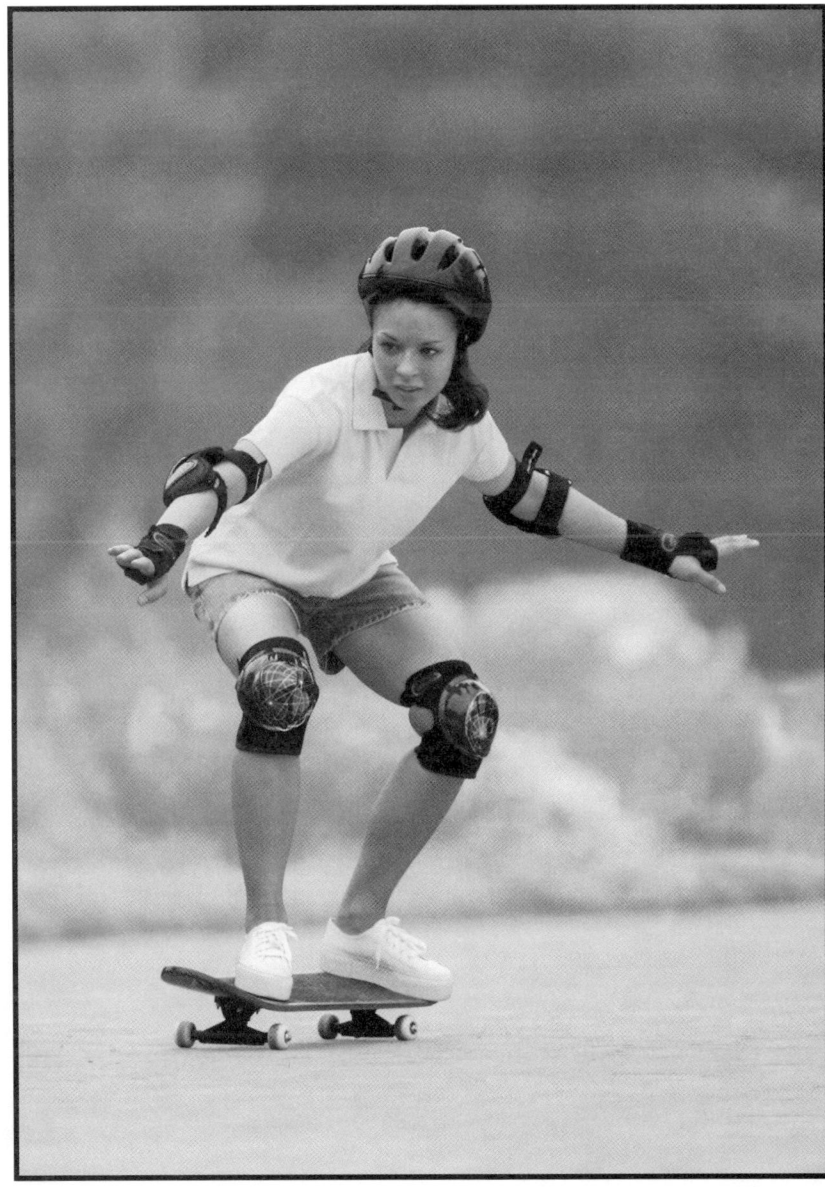

PHOTO CREDITS
Cover Photo: KS Studios

SRA/McGraw-Hill
A Division of The McGraw-Hill Companies

2002 Imprint
Copyright © 1999 by SRA/McGraw-Hill.

Send all inquiries to:
SRA/McGraw-Hill
8787 Orion Place
Columbus, Ohio 43240-4027

Printed in the United States of America.

R74782.01

13 14   MAZ 07 06 05 04

Student _________________________ Teacher _________________________ Date _____________

	Skills tested		Number of errors	Pass criterion	Pass + Fail 0	If failed, review these lessons.
GROUP SECTION		**WORD IDENTIFICATION**				
	1	Writing Letters for Sounds		Pass if 0–1 error		27–30
	2	Writing Words without Endings		Pass if 0 errors		23, 25, 27, 29
	3	Matching Completion		Pass if 0 errors		1–4
	4	Sentence Copying		Pass if 0 errors		1–3
INDIVIDUAL SECTION	5	Short-Vowel Words		Pass if 0–1 error		1–9, 15, 16, 20, 25
	6	Long-Vowel Words		Pass if 0–1 error		6, 8–10, 24–26
	7	Sound Combinations		Pass if 0–1 error		1–9, 34, 35
	8	Word Endings *ed, ly, er*		Pass if 0–1 error		23, 26, 28–35
	9	Irregular Words		Pass if 0–1 error		27, 29–31
		STORY READING	**Time**			
	10	Rate (Time)		Pass if 80 secs. or less		28–35
	11	Accuracy (Errors)		Pass if 0–4 errors		28–35
	12	Comprehension		Pass if 0–1 error		28–35

TEST 1

1

_______ _______ _______ _______ _______

_______ _______ _______ _______ _______

2 The words in the first column have endings.
Write the same words without endings in the second column.

raked

dropping

nearly

shortest

grinned

3 Match the words and complete them.

beaten   fe

trash   ing

road   en

sleeping   sh

felt   r

4 Copy this sentence:
The tramp gets in shape.

____

Individual Section

5   pack   fell   ramp   win   dug

     not   get   bum   pit   drop

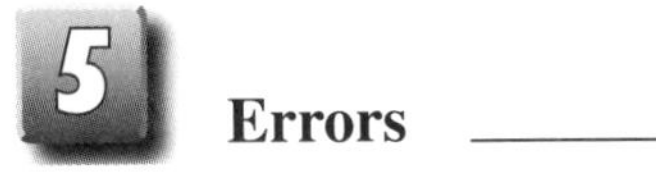

6   gate   hope   time   week   rider

     nose   fake   wheel   like   shape

7   holds   meal   sore   ranch   load

     reach   horse   board   coldest   heaps

8   sweeping   hammer   yearly   grinned   likely

     stayed   mopping   handed   popper   bigger

8   Errors ______

9   minutes   any   people   couldn't   money

9   Errors ______

10

The tramp was getting in shape. When he got up, the sun was coming up over the hill in the east. When he went to bed, the sun was dropping in the west. He worked and worked every day. He sheared sheep. He made gates and pens for pigs. He dug holes for trees. He was getting thinner and thinner.

The tramp had stayed at the ranch for ten weeks. He told the rancher, "I need more meat and beans." "Yes," she said. "You have worked and worked. You are faster and thinner. You may have more meat and beans.

10 Time _____________   **11** Errors _______

12

Record student's answers here:

1. When did the tramp go to bed?

   ____

2. Name 2 things the tramp did for work at the ranch.

   ____

3. How long did the tramp stay at the ranch?

   ____

4. What did the tramp tell the rancher he needed?

   ____

5. Did the tramp get more to eat?

   ____

12 Errors _______

DECODING B1 MASTERY TEST 2
STUDENT PROFILE

Student _______________________ Teacher _______________________ Date _______________

			Number of errors	Pass criterion	Pass + Fail 0	If failed, review these lessons.
GROUP SECTION	**WORD IDENTIFICATION**					
	1	Identifying Letter Combinations		Pass if 0–1 error		40, 44, 45
	2	Writing Words without Endings		Pass if 0–1 error		52, 58–60
	3	Following Instructions		Pass if 0 errors		46, 47, 56
INDIVIDUAL SECTION	**4**	Writing Compound Words		Pass if 0 errors		37–40, 42–45, 48, 62
	5	Short-Vowel Words		Pass if 0–1 error		49, 51–53, 59
	6	Consonant Digraphs		Pass if 0–1 error		9, 12, 47, 48, 52
	7	*ed* Endings in Short-Vowel Words		Pass if 0–1 error		13, 49, 58–61
	8	Word Endings *s, ing, est, er,* and *ery*		Pass if 0–1 error		27, 31, 45, 49, 63, 64
	9	Sound Combinations *ai, oa, or, ol, ea, ou, ow*		Pass if 0–2 errors		51, 52, 55, 61, 62
	10	Irregular Words		Pass if 0–1 error		50, 57–63
	STORY READING	**Time**				
	11	Rate (Time)		Pass if 80 secs. or less		61–65
	12	Accuracy (Errors)		Pass if 0–4 errors		61–65
	13	Comprehension		Pass if 0–1 error		61–65

TEST 2

 **Cross out the words that don't have wh.**

where	with	that	when	how	wheel
word	then	what	why	week	who

 **The words in the first column have endings.**
Write the same words without endings in the second column.

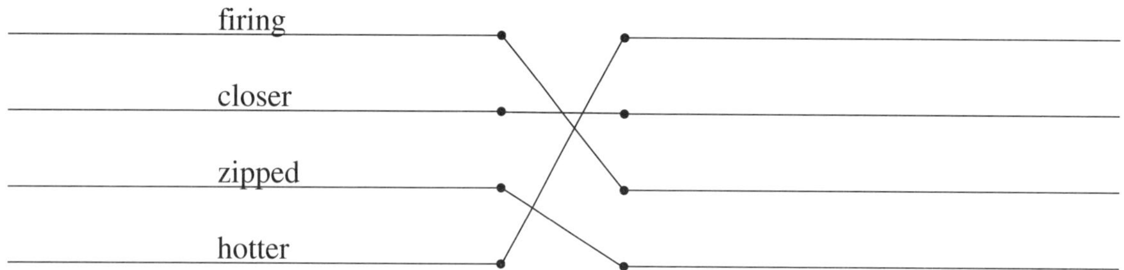

firing

closer

zipped

hotter

 Write the word **louder.** Make a line over **loud.** ___________________________

Write the word **first.** Make a line under **ir.** ___________________________

Write the words.

may	+	be	=	__________
any	+	body	=	__________
near	+	ly	=	__________
her	+	self	=	__________

Individual Section

5 | plop | list | gum | dress | tramp
| stand | crest | pond | fix | must

5 Errors ______

6 | smash | when | chips | shop | things
| whisper | there | fresh | wheels | brush

6 Errors ______

7 | dressed | pinned | spotted | happened | handed
| dragged | lifted | zipped | stepped | slammed

7 Errors ______

8 | trying | plants | bragging | feels | slaps
| fastest | slippery | campers | slowest | teller

8 Errors ______

9 | main | please | boards | form | bolt
| painted | beat | grow | older | croak
| could | loud | should | mouth | ouch

9 Errors ______

10 together   because   private   difference   done

what   millions   brother   know   who

10 Errors _______

11

People were going in a ship from one land to another. They were sailing the sea when a bolt came out of the ship. And the ship began to sink. Men, women, and dogs were in the water. People were swimming and shouting. But the people and dogs were not sinking. They were holding on to boards. They yelled and yelled. One man did not yell. He whispered. This is what that man said, "I can't swim."

The other people grabbed on to him and kept him from sinking. Then a boat came by. A few people dragged him to the boat. When everybody was in the boat, they went to shore. They went faster and faster. They were saved.

11 Time _______________

12 Errors _______

13 *Record student's answers here:*

1. Why did the ship begin to sink?

____

2. Why did the people not sink?

____

3. What did the one man whisper? _______________________________

4. How did the people help him?

____

5. Where did they go in the boat? _______________________________

13 Errors _______

Decoding Strategies

**Mastery Test Booklet
Decoding B1**

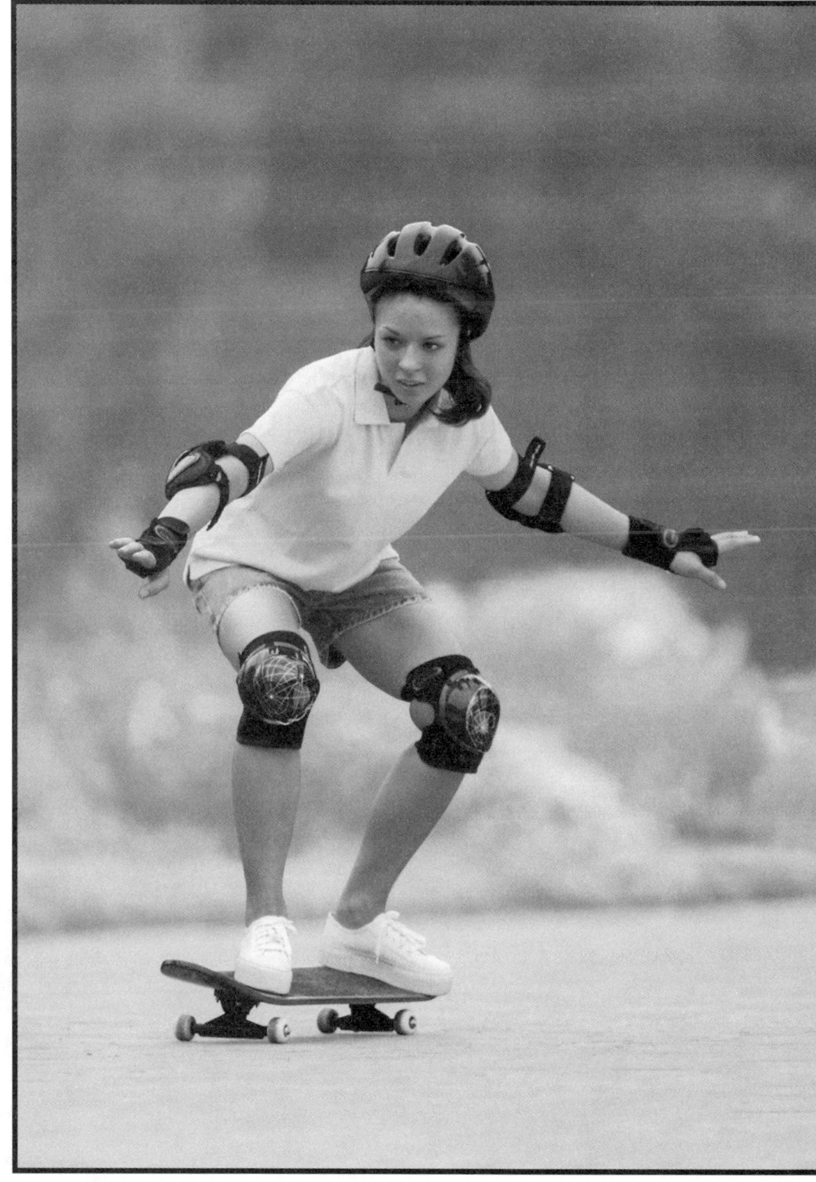

PHOTO CREDITS
Cover Photo: KS Studios

SRA/McGraw-Hill
A Division of The McGraw-Hill Companies

2002 Imprint
Copyright © 1999 by SRA/McGraw-Hill.

Send all inquiries to:
SRA/McGraw-Hill
8787 Orion Place
Columbus, Ohio 43240-4027

Printed in the United States of America.

R74782.01

   13 14   MAZ 07 06 05 04

DECODING B1 MASTERY TEST 1
STUDENT PROFILE

Student ______________________ Teacher ______________________ Date ______________________

	Skills tested	Number of errors	Pass criterion	Pass + Fail 0	If failed, review these lessons.
GROUP SECTION	**WORD IDENTIFICATION**				
	1 Writing Letters for Sounds		Pass if 0–1 error		27–30
	2 Writing Words without Endings		Pass if 0 errors		23, 25, 27, 29
	3 Matching Completion		Pass if 0 errors		1–4
	4 Sentence Copying		Pass if 0 errors		1–3
INDIVIDUAL SECTION	**5** Short-Vowel Words		Pass if 0–1 error		1–9, 15, 16, 20, 25
	6 Long-Vowel Words		Pass if 0–1 error		6, 8–10, 24–26
	7 Sound Combinations		Pass if 0–1 error		1–9, 34, 35
	8 Word Endings *ed, ly, er*		Pass if 0–1 error		23, 26, 28–35
	9 Irregular Words		Pass if 0–1 error		27, 29–31
	STORY READING — Time				
	10 Rate (Time)		Pass if 80 secs. or less		28–35
	11 Accuracy (Errors)		Pass if 0–4 errors		28–35
	12 Comprehension		Pass if 0–1 error		28–35

TEST 1

1

___________ ___________ ___________ ___________ ___________

___________ ___________ ___________ ___________ ___________

2 The words in the first column have endings.
Write the same words without endings in the second column.

raked

dropping

nearly

shortest

grinned

3 Match the words and complete them.

beaten   fe

trash   ing

road   en

sleeping   sh

felt   r

4 Copy this sentence:
The tramp gets in shape.

____

5 pack fell ramp win dug
   not get bum pit drop

5 Errors _______

6 gate hope time week rider
   nose fake wheel like shape

6 Errors _______

7 holds meal sore ranch load
   reach horse board coldest heaps

7 Errors _______

8 sweeping hammer yearly grinned likely
   stayed mopping handed popper bigger

8 Errors _______

9 minutes any people couldn't money

9 Errors _______

10

The tramp was getting in shape. When he got up, the sun was coming up over the hill in the east. When he went to bed, the sun was dropping in the west. He worked and worked every day. He sheared sheep. He made gates and pens for pigs. He dug holes for trees. He was getting thinner and thinner.

The tramp had stayed at the ranch for ten weeks. He told the rancher, "I need more meat and beans." "Yes," she said. "You have worked and worked. You are faster and thinner. You may have more meat and beans.

10 Time ___________   **11** Errors ______

12

Record student's answers here:

1. When did the tramp go to bed?

____

2. Name 2 things the tramp did for work at the ranch.

____

3. How long did the tramp stay at the ranch?

____

4. What did the tramp tell the rancher he needed?

____

5. Did the tramp get more to eat?

____

12 Errors ______

DECODING B1 MASTERY TEST 2
STUDENT PROFILE

Student ______________________ Teacher ______________________ Date ______________

	Skills tested		Number of errors	Pass criterion	Pass + Fail 0	If failed, review these lessons.
GROUP SECTION	**WORD IDENTIFICATION**					
	1 Identifying Letter Combinations			Pass if 0–1 error		40, 44, 45
	2 Writing Words without Endings			Pass if 0–1 error		52, 58–60
	3 Following Instructions			Pass if 0 errors		46, 47, 56
INDIVIDUAL SECTION	**4** Writing Compound Words			Pass if 0 errors		37–40, 42–45, 48, 62
	5 Short-Vowel Words			Pass if 0–1 error		49, 51–53, 59
	6 Consonant Digraphs			Pass if 0–1 error		9, 12, 47, 48, 52
	7 *ed* Endings in Short-Vowel Words			Pass if 0–1 error		13, 49, 58–61
	8 Word Endings *s, ing, est, er,* and *ery*			Pass if 0–1 error		27, 31, 45, 49, 63, 64
	9 Sound Combinations *ai, oa, or, ol, ea, ou, ow*			Pass if 0–2 errors		51, 52, 55, 61, 62
	10 Irregular Words			Pass if 0–1 error		50, 57–63
	STORY READING	**Time**				
	11 Rate (Time)			Pass if 80 secs. or less		61–65
	12 Accuracy (Errors)			Pass if 0–4 errors		61–65
	13 Comprehension			Pass if 0–1 error		61–65

TEST 2

 **1** Cross out the words that don't have **wh.**

where with that when how wheel

word then what why week who

 **2** The words in the first column have endings.
Write the same words without endings in the second column.

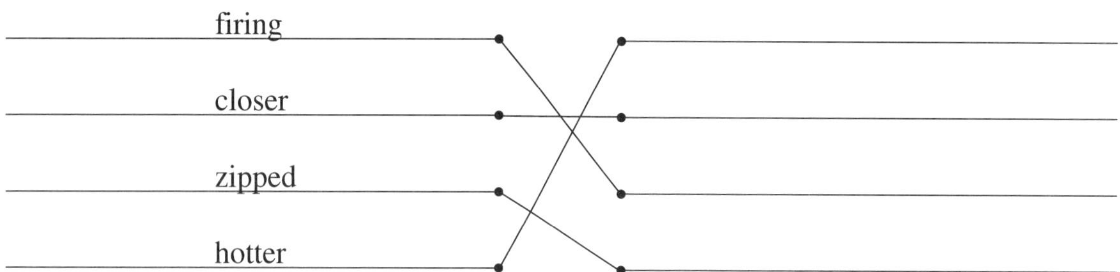

firing

closer

zipped

hotter

 **3** Write the word **louder.** Make a line over **loud.** ___________________________

Write the word **first.** Make a line under **ir.** ___________________________

4 Write the words.

may	+	be	=	
any	+	body	=	
near	+	ly	=	
her	+	self	=	

Individual Section

5 | plop · list · gum · dress · tramp
stand · crest · pond · fix · must

5 Errors ______

6 | smash · when · chips · shop · things
whisper · there · fresh · wheels · brush

6 Errors ______

7 | dressed · pinned · spotted · happened · handed
dragged · lifted · zipped · stepped · slammed

7 Errors ______

8 | trying · plants · bragging · feels · slaps
fastest · slippery · campers · slowest · teller

8 Errors ______

9 | main · please · boards · form · bolt
painted · beat · grow · older · croak
could · loud · should · mouth · ouch

9 Errors ______

together   because   private   difference   done

what   millions   brother   know   who

11

People were going in a ship from one land to another. They were sailing the sea when a bolt came out of the ship. And the ship began to sink. Men, women, and dogs were in the water. People were swimming and shouting. But the people and dogs were not sinking. They were holding on to boards. They yelled and yelled. One man did not yell. He whispered. This is what that man said, "I can't swim."

The other people grabbed on to him and kept him from sinking. Then a boat came by. A few people dragged him to the boat. When everybody was in the boat, they went to shore. They went faster and faster. They were saved.

11 Time _______________   **12** Errors _______

13 *Record student's answers here:*

1. Why did the ship begin to sink?

____

2. Why did the people not sink?

____

3. What did the one man whisper? _________________________________

4. How did the people help him?

____

5. Where did they go in the boat? _________________________________

13 Errors _______

Decoding Strategies

**Mastery Test Booklet
Decoding B1**

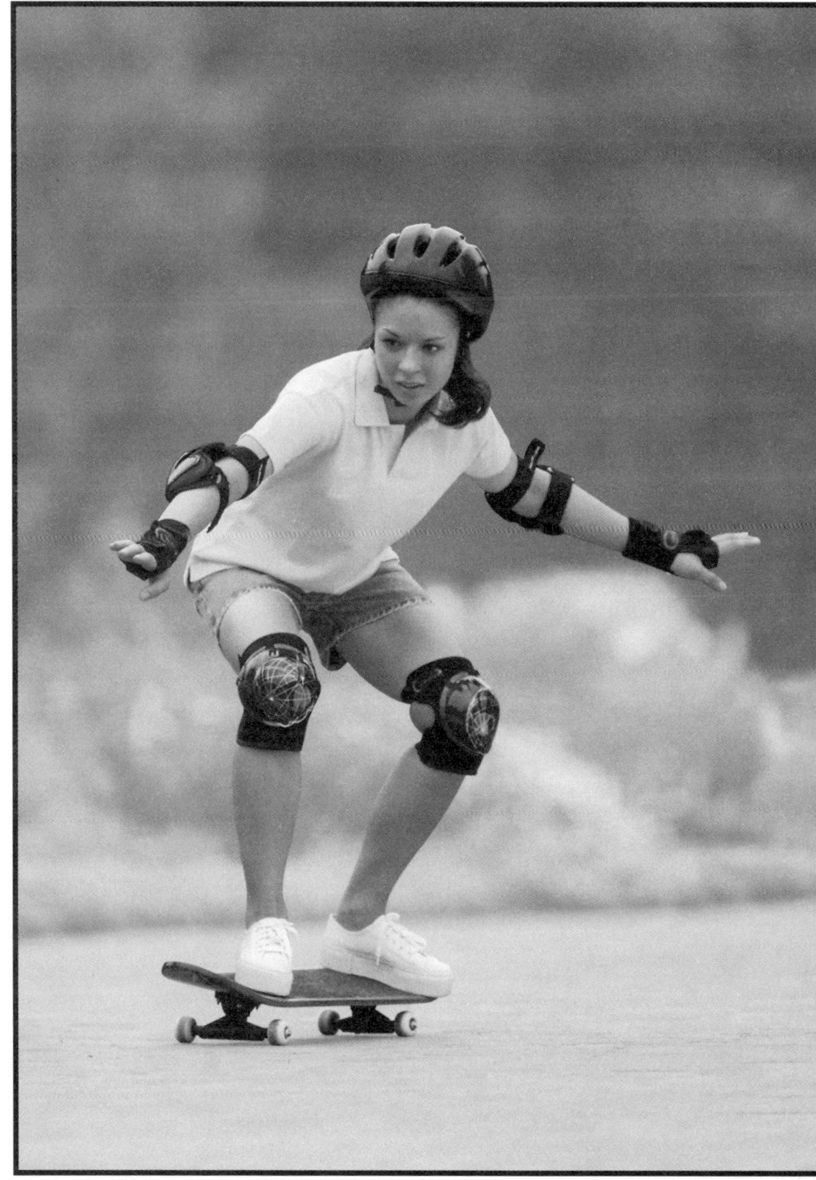

SRA/McGraw-Hill

A Division of The McGraw·Hill Companies

2002 Imprint
Copyright © 1999 by SRA/McGraw-Hill.

Send all inquiries to:
SRA/McGraw-Hill
8787 Orion Place
Columbus, Ohio 43240-4027

Printed in the United States of America.

R74782.01

13 14   MAZ 07 06 05 04

DECODING B1 MASTERY TEST 1
STUDENT PROFILE

Student ____________________   **Teacher** ____________________   **Date** ____________________

	Skills tested		Number of errors	Pass criterion	Pass + Fail 0	If failed, review these lessons.
GROUP SECTION						
	WORD IDENTIFICATION					
	1	Writing Letters for Sounds		Pass if 0–1 error		27–30
	2	Writing Words without Endings		Pass if 0 errors		23, 25, 27, 29
	3	Matching Completion		Pass if 0 errors		1–4
	4	Sentence Copying		Pass if 0 errors		1–3
INDIVIDUAL SECTION	**5**	Short-Vowel Words		Pass if 0–1 error		1–9, 15, 16, 20, 25
	6	Long-Vowel Words		Pass if 0–1 error		6, 8–10, 24–26
	7	Sound Combinations		Pass if 0–1 error		1–9, 34, 35
	8	Word Endings *ed, ly, er*		Pass if 0–1 error		23, 26, 28–35
	9	Irregular Words		Pass if 0–1 error		27, 29–31
	STORY READING	Time				
	10	Rate (Time)		Pass if 80 secs. or less		28–35
	11	Accuracy (Errors)		Pass if 0–4 errors		28–35
	12	Comprehension		Pass if 0–1 error		28–35

TEST 1

1

______ ______ ______ ______ ______

______ ______ ______ ______ ______

2 The words in the first column have endings.
Write the same words without endings in the second column.

raked

dropping

nearly

shortest

grinned

3 Match the words and complete them.

beaten	fe
trash	ing
road	en
sleeping	sh
felt	r

4 Copy this sentence:
The tramp gets in shape.

____

Individual Section

5   pack   fell   ramp   win   dug

not   get   bum   pit   drop

6   gate   hope   time   week   rider

nose   fake   wheel   like   shape

7   holds   meal   sore   ranch   load

reach   horse   board   coldest   heaps

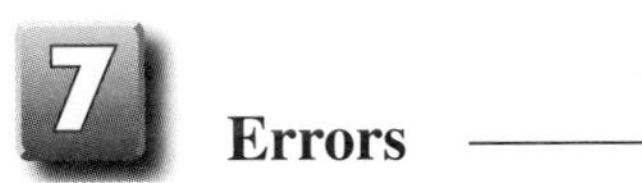

8   sweeping   hammer   yearly   grinned   likely

stayed   mopping   handed   popper   bigger

8   Errors ______

9   minutes   any   people   couldn't   money

9   Errors ______

The tramp was getting in shape. When he got up, the sun was coming up over the hill in the east. When he went to bed, the sun was dropping in the west. He worked and worked every day. He sheared sheep. He made gates and pens for pigs. He dug holes for trees. He was getting thinner and thinner.

The tramp had stayed at the ranch for ten weeks. He told the rancher, "I need more meat and beans." "Yes," she said. "You have worked and worked. You are faster and thinner. You may have more meat and beans.

10 Time _____________   **11** Errors _______

12

Record student's answers here:

1. When did the tramp go to bed?

   ____

2. Name 2 things the tramp did for work at the ranch.

   ____

3. How long did the tramp stay at the ranch?

   ____

4. What did the tramp tell the rancher he needed?

   ____

5. Did the tramp get more to eat?

   ____

12 Errors _______

DECODING B1 MASTERY TEST 2
STUDENT PROFILE

Student ________________________   **Teacher** ________________________   **Date** ________________

	Skills tested		Number of errors	Pass criterion	Pass + Fail 0	If failed, review these lessons.
GROUP SECTION	**WORD IDENTIFICATION**					
	1	Identifying Letter Combinations		Pass if 0–1 error		40, 44, 45
	2	Writing Words without Endings		Pass if 0–1 error		52, 58–60
	3	Following Instructions		Pass if 0 errors		46, 47, 56
INDIVIDUAL SECTION	4	Writing Compound Words		Pass if 0 errors		37–40, 42–45, 48, 62
	5	Short-Vowel Words		Pass if 0–1 error		49, 51–53, 59
	6	Consonant Digraphs		Pass if 0–1 error		9, 12, 47, 48, 52
	7	*ed* Endings in Short-Vowel Words		Pass if 0–1 error		13, 49, 58–61
	8	Word Endings *s, ing, est, er,* and *ery*		Pass if 0–1 error		27, 31, 45, 49, 63, 64
	9	Sound Combinations *ai, oa, or, ol, ea, ou, ow*		Pass if 0–2 errors		51, 52, 55, 61, 62
	10	Irregular Words		Pass if 0–1 error		50, 57–63
	STORY READING	**Time**				
	11	Rate (Time)		Pass if 80 secs. or less		61–65
	12	Accuracy (Errors)		Pass if 0–4 errors		61–65
	13	Comprehension		Pass if 0–1 error		61–65

TEST 2

 **1** Cross out the words that don't have **wh.**

where   with   that   when   how   wheel

word   then   what   why   week   who

 **2** The words in the first column have endings.
Write the same words without endings in the second column.

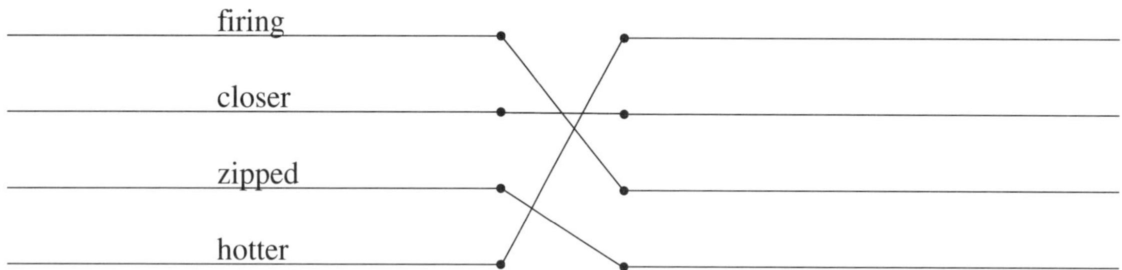

firing

closer

zipped

hotter

 **3** Write the word **louder.** Make a line over **loud.** ___________________

Write the word **first.** Make a line under **ir.** ___________________

 **4** Write the words.

may	+	be	=
any	+	body	=
near	+	ly	=
her	+	self	=

Individual Section

| **5** | plop | list | gum | dress | tramp | | **5** Errors _______ |
| | stand | crest | pond | fix | must | | |

| **6** | smash | when | chips | shop | things | | **6** Errors _______ |
| | whisper | there | fresh | wheels | brush | | |

| **7** | dressed | pinned | spotted | happened | handed | | **7** Errors _______ |
| | dragged | lifted | zipped | stepped | slammed | | |

| **8** | trying | plants | bragging | feels | slaps | | **8** Errors _______ |
| | fastest | slippery | campers | slowest | teller | | |

9	main	please	boards	form	bolt		
	painted	beat	grow	older	croak		**9** Errors _______
	could	loud	should	mouth	ouch		

together	because	private	difference	done
what	millions	brother	know	who

10 Errors _______

11

People were going in a ship from one land to another. They were sailing the sea when a bolt came out of the ship. And the ship began to sink. Men, women, and dogs were in the water. People were swimming and shouting. But the people and dogs were not sinking. They were holding on to boards. They yelled and yelled. One man did not yell. He whispered. This is what that man said, "I can't swim."

The other people grabbed on to him and kept him from sinking. Then a boat came by. A few people dragged him to the boat. When everybody was in the boat, they went to shore. They went faster and faster. They were saved.

11 Time _______________   **12** Errors _______

13 *Record student's answers here:*

1. Why did the ship begin to sink?

   ____

2. Why did the people not sink?

   ____

3. What did the one man whisper? _______________________

4. How did the people help him?

   ____

5. Where did they go in the boat? _______________________

13 Errors _______

Decoding Strategies

Mastery Test Booklet
Decoding B1

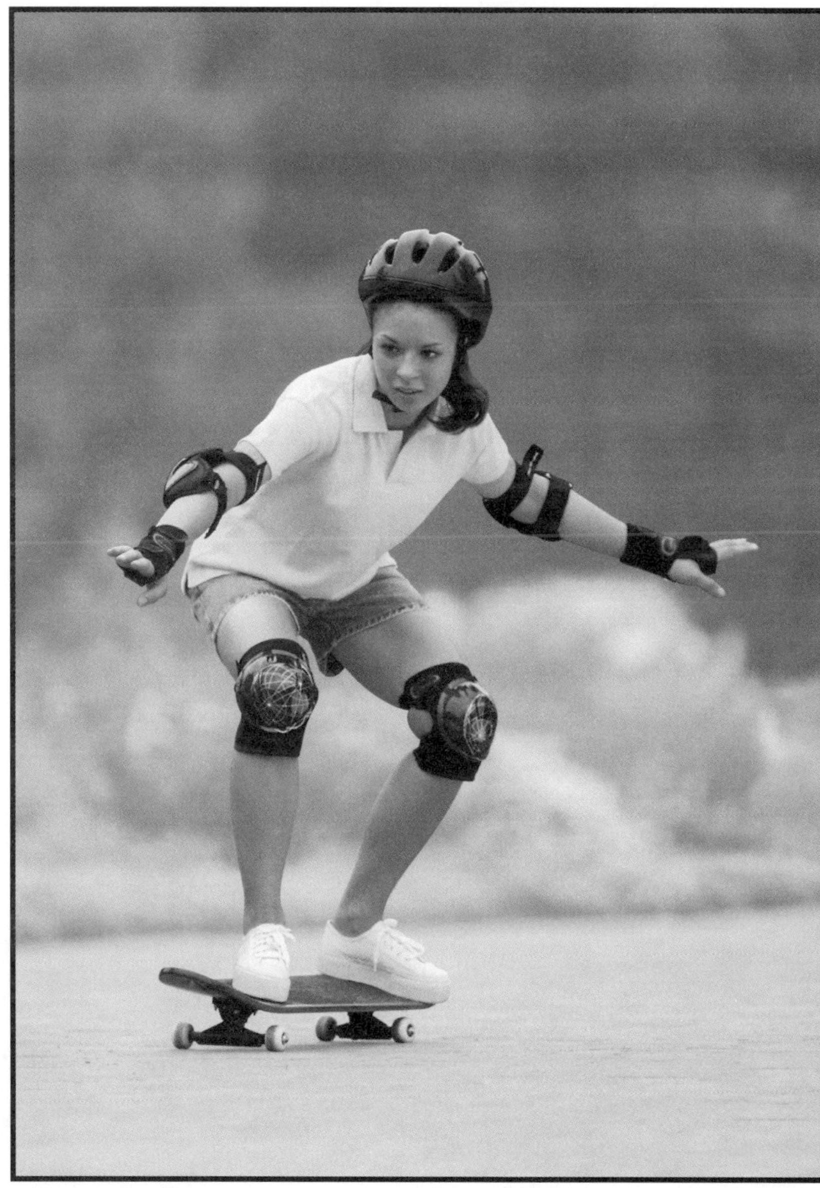

PHOTO CREDITS
Cover Photo: KS Studios

SRA/McGraw-Hill

A Division of The McGraw-Hill Companies

2002 Imprint
Copyright © 1999 by SRA/McGraw-Hill.

Send all inquiries to:
SRA/McGraw-Hill
8787 Orion Place
Columbus, Ohio 43240-4027

Printed in the United States of America.

R74782.01

13 14   MAZ 07 06 05 04

DECODING B1 MASTERY TEST 1
STUDENT PROFILE

Student _______________________ **Teacher** _______________________ **Date** _______________

	Skills tested		Number of errors	Pass criterion	Pass + Fail 0	If failed, review these lessons.
GROUP SECTION	**WORD IDENTIFICATION**					
	1 Writing Letters for Sounds			Pass if 0–1 error		27–30
	2 Writing Words without Endings			Pass if 0 errors		23, 25, 27, 29
	3 Matching Completion			Pass if 0 errors		1–4
	4 Sentence Copying			Pass if 0 errors		1–3
INDIVIDUAL SECTION	**5** Short-Vowel Words			Pass if 0–1 error		1–9, 15, 16, 20, 25
	6 Long-Vowel Words			Pass if 0–1 error		6, 8–10, 24–26
	7 Sound Combinations			Pass if 0–1 error		1–9, 34, 35
	8 Word Endings *ed, ly, er*			Pass if 0–1 error		23, 26, 28–35
	9 Irregular Words			Pass if 0–1 error		27, 29–31
	STORY READING	**Time**				
	10 Rate (Time)			Pass if 80 secs. or less		28–35
	11 Accuracy (Errors)			Pass if 0–4 errors		28–35
	12 Comprehension			Pass if 0–1 error		28–35

TEST 1

NAME ___________________________________

1

___________ ___________ ___________ ___________ ___________

___________ ___________ ___________ ___________ ___________

2 The words in the first column have endings.
Write the same words without endings in the second column.

raked

dropping

nearly

shortest

grinned

3 Match the words and complete them.

beaten   fe

trash   ing

road   en

sleeping   sh

felt   r

4 Copy this sentence:
The tramp gets in shape.

____

Individual Section

5   pack   fell   ramp   win   dug

      not   get   bum   pit   drop

5   Errors _______

6   gate   hope   time   week   rider

      nose   fake   wheel   like   shape

6   Errors _______

7   holds   meal   sore   ranch   load

      reach   horse   board   coldest   heaps

7   Errors _______

8   sweeping   hammer   yearly   grinned   likely

      stayed   mopping   handed   popper   bigger

8   Errors _______

9   minutes   any   people   couldn't   money

9   Errors _______

The tramp was getting in shape. When he got up, the sun was coming up over the hill in the east. When he went to bed, the sun was dropping in the west. He worked and worked every day. He sheared sheep. He made gates and pens for pigs. He dug holes for trees. He was getting thinner and thinner.

The tramp had stayed at the ranch for ten weeks. He told the rancher, "I need more meat and beans." "Yes," she said. "You have worked and worked. You are faster and thinner. You may have more meat and beans.

10 Time __________   **11** Errors ______

12

Record student's answers here:

1. When did the tramp go to bed?

   ____

2. Name 2 things the tramp did for work at the ranch.

   ____

3. How long did the tramp stay at the ranch?

   ____

4. What did the tramp tell the rancher he needed?

   ____

5. Did the tramp get more to eat?

   ____

12 Errors ______

Student _________________________ Teacher _________________________ Date _____________

	Skills tested	Number of errors	Pass criterion	Pass + Fail 0	If failed, review these lessons.
GROUP SECTION	**WORD IDENTIFICATION**				
	1 Identifying Letter Combinations		Pass if 0–1 error		40, 44, 45
	2 Writing Words without Endings		Pass if 0–1 error		52, 58–60
	3 Following Instructions		Pass if 0 errors		46, 47, 56
INDIVIDUAL SECTION	**4** Writing Compound Words		Pass if 0 errors		37–40, 42–45, 48, 62
	5 Short-Vowel Words		Pass if 0–1 error		49, 51–53, 59
	6 Consonant Digraphs		Pass if 0–1 error		9, 12, 47, 48, 52
	7 *ed* Endings in Short-Vowel Words		Pass if 0–1 error		13, 49, 58–61
	8 Word Endings *s, ing, est, er,* and *ery*		Pass if 0–1 error		27, 31, 45, 49, 63, 64
	9 Sound Combinations *ai, oa, or, ol, ea, ou, ow*		Pass if 0–2 errors		51, 52, 55, 61, 62
	10 Irregular Words		Pass if 0–1 error		50, 57–63
	STORY READING — Time				
	11 Rate (Time)		Pass if 80 secs. or less		61–65
	12 Accuracy (Errors)		Pass if 0–4 errors		61–65
	13 Comprehension		Pass if 0–1 error		61–65

TEST 2

 Cross out the words that don't have **wh.**

where   with   that   when   how   wheel

word   then   what   why   week   who

 The words in the first column have endings.
Write the same words without endings in the second column.

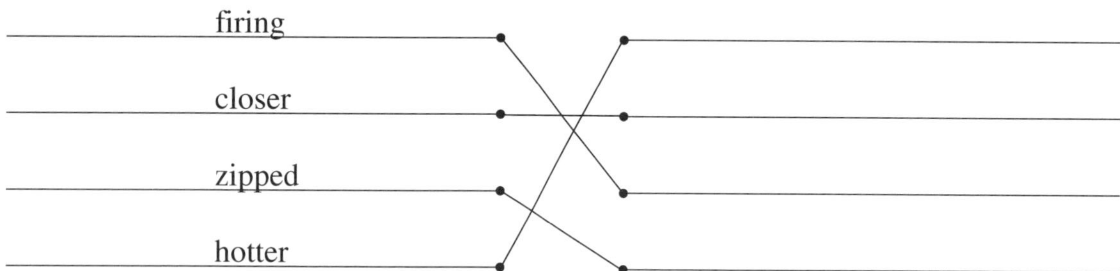

firing

closer

zipped

hotter

 Write the word **louder.** Make a line over **loud.** ______________________

Write the word **first.** Make a line under **ir.** ______________________

 Write the words.

______ may ______ + ______ be ______ = ______________________

______ any ______ + ______ body ______ = ______________________

______ near ______ + ______ ly ______ = ______________________

______ her ______ + ______ self ______ = ______________________

Individual Section

5 | plop | list | gum | dress | tramp
    stand | crest | pond | fix | must

5 Errors ______

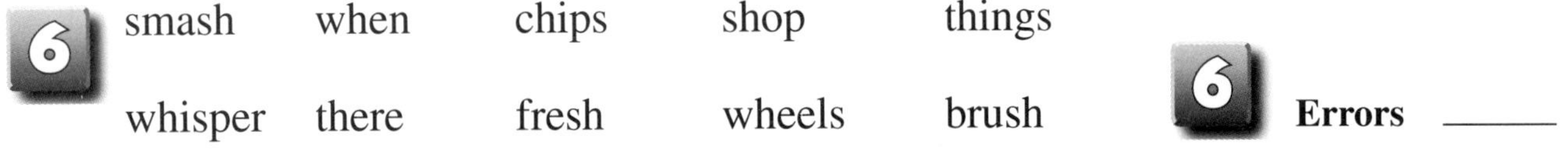

6 | smash | when | chips | shop | things
    whisper | there | fresh | wheels | brush

6 Errors ______

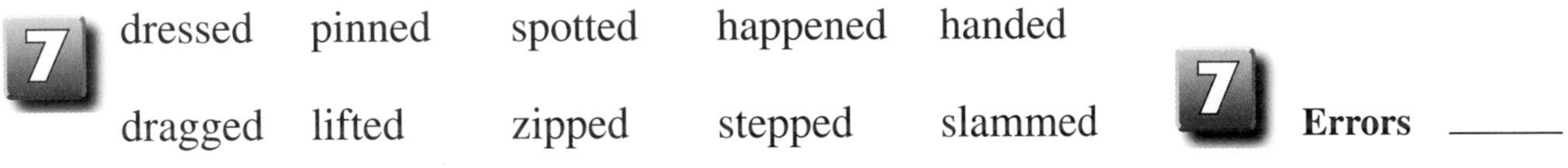

7 | dressed | pinned | spotted | happened | handed
    dragged | lifted | zipped | stepped | slammed

7 Errors ______

8 | trying | plants | bragging | feels | slaps
    fastest | slippery | campers | slowest | teller

8 Errors ______

9 | main | please | boards | form | bolt
    painted | beat | grow | older | croak
    could | loud | should | mouth | ouch

9 Errors ______

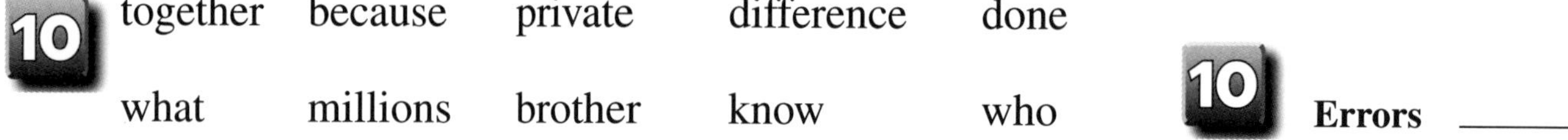

10 together   because   private   difference   done

what   millions   brother   know   who

10 Errors ______

11

People were going in a ship from one land to another. They were sailing the sea when a bolt came out of the ship. And the ship began to sink. Men, women, and dogs were in the water. People were swimming and shouting. But the people and dogs were not sinking. They were holding on to boards. They yelled and yelled. One man did not yell. He whispered. This is what that man said, "I can't swim."

The other people grabbed on to him and kept him from sinking. Then a boat came by. A few people dragged him to the boat. When everybody was in the boat, they went to shore. They went faster and faster. They were saved.

11 Time ______________   **12** Errors ______

13 *Record student's answers here:*

1. Why did the ship begin to sink?

____

2. Why did the people not sink?

____

3. What did the one man whisper? _____________________________

4. How did the people help him?

____

5. Where did they go in the boat? ____________________________

13 Errors ______

Decoding Strategies

Mastery Test Booklet
Decoding B1

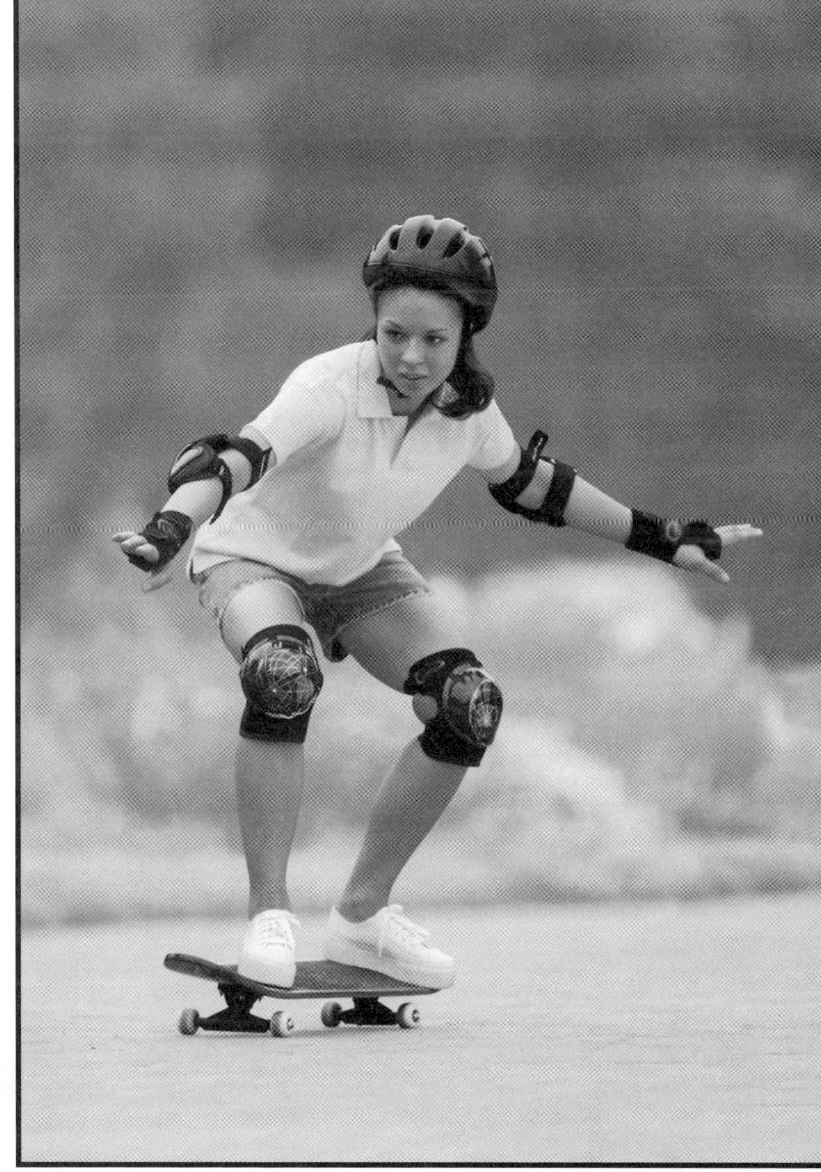

PHOTO CREDITS
Cover Photo: KS Studios

SRA/McGraw-Hill

A Division of The McGraw·Hill Companies

2002 Imprint
Copyright © 1999 by SRA/McGraw-Hill.

Send all inquiries to:
SRA/McGraw-Hill
8787 Orion Place
Columbus, Ohio 43240-4027

Printed in the United States of America.

R74782.01

13 14   MAZ 07 06 05 04

DECODING B1 MASTERY TEST 1
STUDENT PROFILE

Student _________________________ Teacher _________________________ Date _______________

<table>
<tr><td rowspan="2"></td><td rowspan="2">Skills tested</td><td colspan="2"></td><td>Number
of errors</td><td>Pass
criterion</td><td>Pass +
Fail 0</td><td>If failed, review
these lessons.</td></tr>
<tr></tr>
<tr><td rowspan="5">GROUP SECTION</td><td colspan="3">WORD IDENTIFICATION</td><td></td><td></td><td></td><td></td></tr>
<tr><td colspan="2">1 Writing Letters for Sounds</td><td></td><td>Pass if
0–1 error</td><td></td><td>27–30</td></tr>
<tr><td colspan="2">2 Writing Words without Endings</td><td></td><td>Pass if
0 errors</td><td></td><td>23, 25, 27, 29</td></tr>
<tr><td colspan="2">3 Matching Completion</td><td></td><td>Pass if
0 errors</td><td></td><td>1–4</td></tr>
<tr><td colspan="2">4 Sentence Copying</td><td></td><td>Pass if
0 errors</td><td></td><td>1–3</td></tr>
<tr><td rowspan="9">INDIVIDUAL SECTION</td><td colspan="2">5 Short-Vowel Words</td><td></td><td>Pass if
0–1 error</td><td></td><td>1–9, 15, 16, 20, 25</td></tr>
<tr><td colspan="2">6 Long-Vowel Words</td><td></td><td>Pass if
0–1 error</td><td></td><td>6, 8–10, 24–26</td></tr>
<tr><td colspan="2">7 Sound Combinations</td><td></td><td>Pass if
0–1 error</td><td></td><td>1–9, 34, 35</td></tr>
<tr><td colspan="2">8 Word Endings ed, ly, er</td><td></td><td>Pass if
0–1 error</td><td></td><td>23, 26, 28–35</td></tr>
<tr><td colspan="2">9 Irregular Words</td><td></td><td>Pass if
0–1 error</td><td></td><td>27, 29–31</td></tr>
<tr><td>STORY READING</td><td>Time</td><td colspan="4"></td></tr>
<tr><td>10 Rate (Time)</td><td></td><td></td><td>Pass if 80
secs. or less</td><td></td><td>28–35</td></tr>
<tr><td>11 Accuracy (Errors)</td><td></td><td></td><td>Pass if
0–4 errors</td><td></td><td>28–35</td></tr>
<tr><td>12 Comprehension</td><td></td><td></td><td>Pass if
0–1 error</td><td></td><td>28–35</td></tr>
</table>

TEST 1

NAME ____

1

______________ ______________ ______________ ______________

______________ ______________ ______________ ______________

2 The words in the first column have endings. Write the same words without endings in the second column.

raked

dropping

nearly

shortest

grinned

3 Match the words and complete them.

beaten   fe

trash   ing

road   en

sleeping   sh

felt   r

4 Copy this sentence:
The tramp gets in shape.

____

Individual Section

5   pack   fell   ramp   win   dug

    not   get   bum   pit   drop

5 Errors ______

6   gate   hope   time   week   rider

    nose   fake   wheel   like   shape

6 Errors ______

7   holds   meal   sore   ranch   load

    reach   horse   board   coldest   heaps

7 Errors ______

8   sweeping   hammer   yearly   grinned   likely

    stayed   mopping   handed   popper   bigger

8 Errors ______

9   minutes   any   people   couldn't   money

9 Errors ______

10

The tramp was getting in shape. When he got up, the sun was coming up over the hill in the east. When he went to bed, the sun was dropping in the west. He worked and worked every day. He sheared sheep. He made gates and pens for pigs. He dug holes for trees. He was getting thinner and thinner.

The tramp had stayed at the ranch for ten weeks. He told the rancher, "I need more meat and beans." "Yes," she said. "You have worked and worked. You are faster and thinner. You may have more meat and beans.

10 Time __________   **11** Errors ______

12

Record student's answers here:

1. When did the tramp go to bed?

   ____

2. Name 2 things the tramp did for work at the ranch.

   ____

3. How long did the tramp stay at the ranch?

   ____

4. What did the tramp tell the rancher he needed?

   ____

5. Did the tramp get more to eat?

   ____

12 Errors ______

DECODING B1 MASTERY TEST 2
STUDENT PROFILE

Student ______________________ **Teacher** ______________________ **Date** ______________

		Skills tested	Number of errors	Pass criterion	Pass + Fail 0	If failed, review these lessons.
GROUP SECTION		**WORD IDENTIFICATION**				
	1	Identifying Letter Combinations		Pass if 0–1 error		40, 44, 45
	2	Writing Words without Endings		Pass if 0–1 error		52, 58–60
	3	Following Instructions		Pass if 0 errors		46, 47, 56
INDIVIDUAL SECTION	4	Writing Compound Words		Pass if 0 errors		37–40, 42–45, 48, 62
	5	Short-Vowel Words		Pass if 0–1 error		49, 51–53, 59
	6	Consonant Digraphs		Pass if 0–1 error		9, 12, 47, 48, 52
	7	*ed* Endings in Short-Vowel Words		Pass if 0–1 error		13, 49, 58–61
	8	Word Endings *s, ing, est, er,* and *ery*		Pass if 0–1 error		27, 31, 45, 49, 63, 64
	9	Sound Combinations *ai, oa, or, ol, ea, ou, ow*		Pass if 0–2 errors		51, 52, 55, 61, 62
	10	Irregular Words		Pass if 0–1 error		50, 57–63
		STORY READING — **Time**				
	11	Rate (Time)		Pass if 80 secs. or less		61–65
	12	Accuracy (Errors)		Pass if 0–4 errors		61–65
	13	Comprehension		Pass if 0–1 error		61–65

TEST 2

 **Cross out the words that don't have wh.**

where   with   that   when   how   wheel

word   then   what   why   week   who

 **The words in the first column have endings.**
Write the same words without endings in the second column.

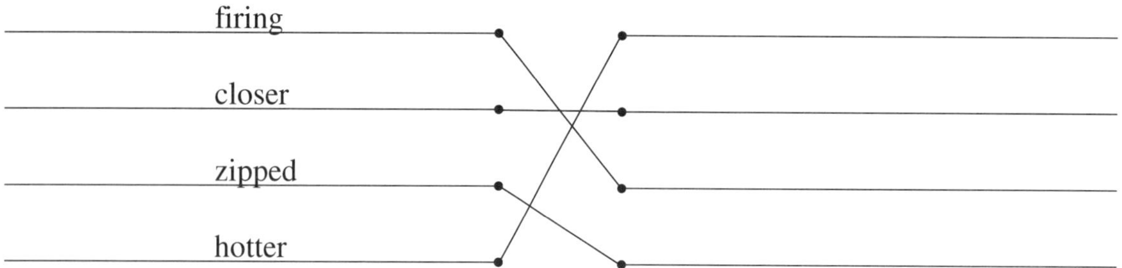

firing

closer

zipped

hotter

3 Write the word **louder.** Make a line over **loud.** _______________________

Write the word **first.** Make a line under **ir.** _______________________

4 Write the words.

may   +   be   = _______________________

any   +   body   = _______________________

near   +   ly   = _______________________

her   +   self   = _______________________

Individual Section

5
| plop | list | gum | dress | tramp |
| stand | crest | pond | fix | must |

5 Errors ______

6
| smash | when | chips | shop | things |
| whisper | there | fresh | wheels | brush |

6 Errors ______

7
| dressed | pinned | spotted | happened | handed |
| dragged | lifted | zipped | stepped | slammed |

7 Errors ______

8
| trying | plants | bragging | feels | slaps |
| fastest | slippery | campers | slowest | teller |

8 Errors ______

9
main	please	boards	form	bolt
painted	beat	grow	older	croak
could	loud	should	mouth	ouch

9 Errors ______

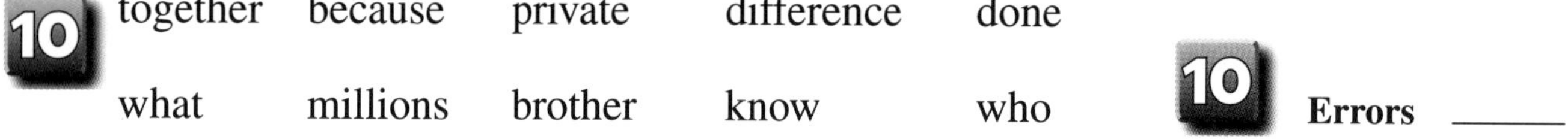

10 together   because   private   difference   done

what   millions   brother   know   who   **10** Errors ______

11

People were going in a ship from one land to another. They were sailing the sea when a bolt came out of the ship. And the ship began to sink. Men, women, and dogs were in the water. People were swimming and shouting. But the people and dogs were not sinking. They were holding on to boards. They yelled and yelled. One man did not yell. He whispered. This is what that man said, "I can't swim."

The other people grabbed on to him and kept him from sinking. Then a boat came by. A few people dragged him to the boat. When everybody was in the boat, they went to shore. They went faster and faster. They were saved.

11 Time ______   **12** Errors ______

13 *Record student's answers here:*

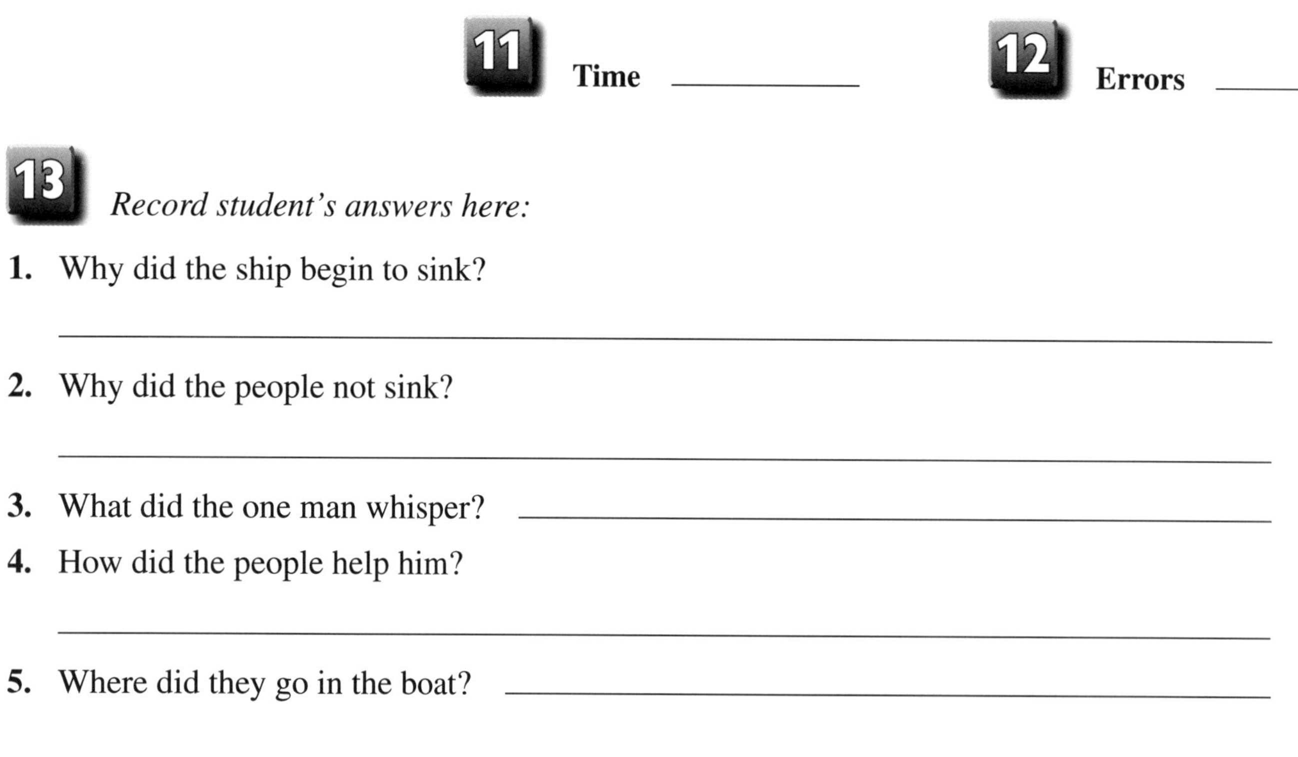

1. Why did the ship begin to sink?

   ____

2. Why did the people not sink?

   ____

3. What did the one man whisper? ____

4. How did the people help him?

   ____

5. Where did they go in the boat? ____

13 Errors ______

Decoding Strategies

Mastery Test Booklet
Decoding B1

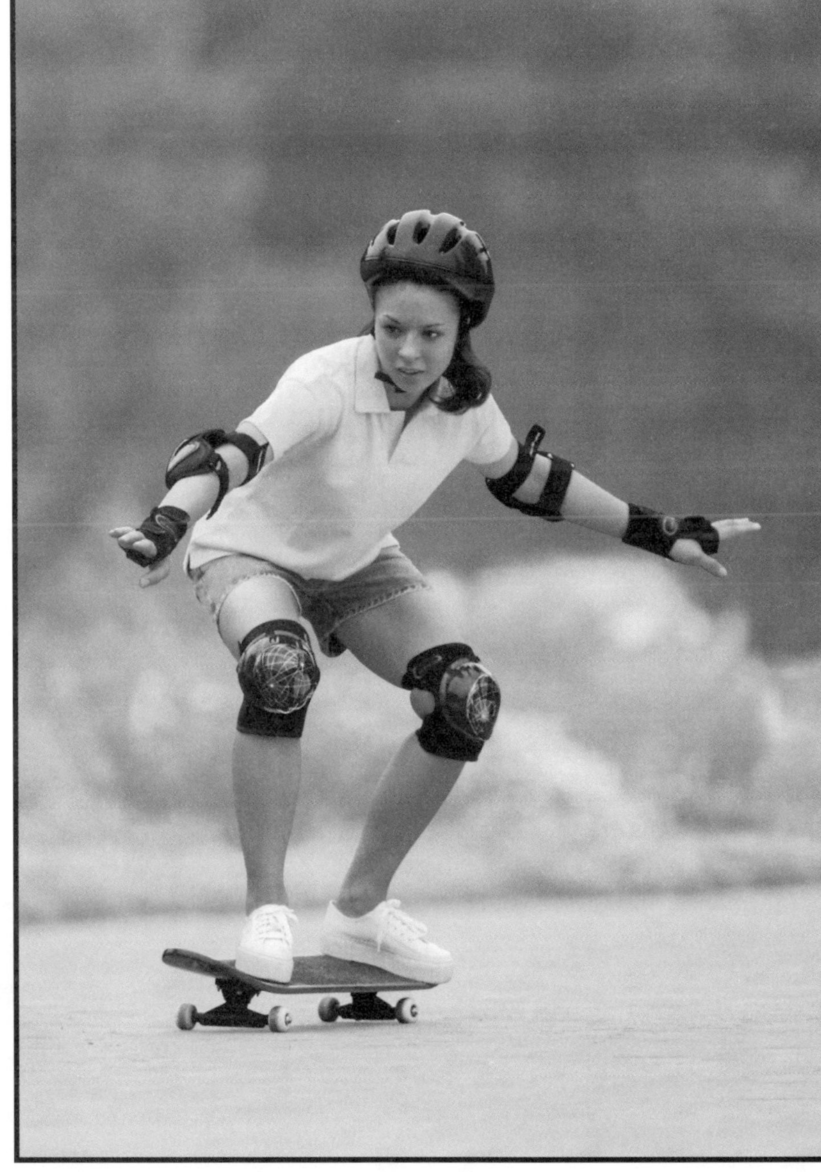

SRA/McGraw-Hill

A Division of The McGraw·Hill Companies

2002 Imprint
Copyright © 1999 by SRA/McGraw-Hill.

Send all inquiries to:
SRA/McGraw-Hill
8787 Orion Place
Columbus, Ohio 43240-4027

Printed in the United States of America.

R74782.01

13 14   MAZ 07 06 05 04

DECODING B1 MASTERY TEST 1
STUDENT PROFILE

Student __________________________ Teacher __________________________ Date ______________

	Skills tested		Number of errors	Pass criterion	Pass + Fail 0	If failed, review these lessons.
GROUP SECTION	**WORD IDENTIFICATION**					
	1 Writing Letters for Sounds			Pass if 0–1 error		27–30
	2 Writing Words without Endings			Pass if 0 errors		23, 25, 27, 29
	3 Matching Completion			Pass if 0 errors		1–4
	4 Sentence Copying			Pass if 0 errors		1–3
INDIVIDUAL SECTION	**5** Short-Vowel Words			Pass if 0–1 error		1–9, 15, 16, 20, 25
	6 Long-Vowel Words			Pass if 0–1 error		6, 8–10, 24–26
	7 Sound Combinations			Pass if 0–1 error		1–9, 34, 35
	8 Word Endings *ed, ly, er*			Pass if 0–1 error		23, 26, 28–35
	9 Irregular Words			Pass if 0–1 error		27, 29–31
	STORY READING	**Time**				
	10 Rate (Time)			Pass if 80 secs. or less		28–35
	11 Accuracy (Errors)			Pass if 0–4 errors		28–35
	12 Comprehension			Pass if 0–1 error		28–35

TEST 1

NAME _______________________________

1

_______ _______ _______ _______

_______ _______ _______ _______

2 The words in the first column have endings.
Write the same words without endings in the second column.

raked

dropping

nearly

shortest

grinned

3 Match the words and complete them.

beaten	fe
trash	ing
road	en
sleeping	sh
felt	r

4 Copy this sentence:
The tramp gets in shape.

____

Individual Section

5
pack   fell   ramp   win   dug
not   get   bum   pit   drop

5 Errors ______

6
gate   hope   time   week   rider
nose   fake   wheel   like   shape

6 Errors ______

7
holds   meal   sore   ranch   load
reach   horse   board   coldest   heaps

7 Errors ______

8
sweeping   hammer   yearly   grinned   likely
stayed   mopping   handed   popper   bigger

8 Errors ______

9
minutes   any   people   couldn't   money

9 Errors ______

10

The tramp was getting in shape. When he got up, the sun was coming up over the hill in the east. When he went to bed, the sun was dropping in the west. He worked and worked every day. He sheared sheep. He made gates and pens for pigs. He dug holes for trees. He was getting thinner and thinner.

The tramp had stayed at the ranch for ten weeks. He told the rancher, "I need more meat and beans." "Yes," she said. "You have worked and worked. You are faster and thinner. You may have more meat and beans.

10 Time _____________   **11** Errors _______

12

Record student's answers here:

1. When did the tramp go to bed?

   ____

2. Name 2 things the tramp did for work at the ranch.

   ____

3. How long did the tramp stay at the ranch?

   ____

4. What did the tramp tell the rancher he needed?

   ____

5. Did the tramp get more to eat?

   ____

12 Errors _______

DECODING B1 MASTERY TEST 2
STUDENT PROFILE

Student _______________________ **Teacher** _______________________ **Date** _______________

	Skills tested		Number of errors	Pass criterion	Pass + Fail 0	If failed, review these lessons.
GROUP SECTION	**WORD IDENTIFICATION**					
	1	Identifying Letter Combinations		Pass if 0–1 error		40, 44, 45
	2	Writing Words without Endings		Pass if 0–1 error		52, 58–60
	3	Following Instructions		Pass if 0 errors		46, 47, 56
INDIVIDUAL SECTION	4	Writing Compound Words		Pass if 0 errors		37–40, 42–45, 48, 62
	5	Short-Vowel Words		Pass if 0–1 error		49, 51–53, 59
	6	Consonant Digraphs		Pass if 0–1 error		9, 12, 47, 48, 52
	7	*ed* Endings in Short-Vowel Words		Pass if 0–1 error		13, 49, 58–61
	8	Word Endings *s, ing, est, er,* and *ery*		Pass if 0–1 error		27, 31, 45, 49, 63, 64
	9	Sound Combinations *ai, oa, or, ol, ea, ou, ow*		Pass if 0–2 errors		51, 52, 55, 61, 62
	10	Irregular Words		Pass if 0–1 error		50, 57–63
	STORY READING	**Time**				
	11	Rate (Time)		Pass if 80 secs. or less		61–65
	12	Accuracy (Errors)		Pass if 0–4 errors		61–65
	13	Comprehension		Pass if 0–1 error		61–65

STUDENT PROFILE TEST 2   5

TEST 2

 **1** Cross out the words that don't have **wh.**

where   with   that   when   how   wheel

word   then   what   why   week   who

 **2** The words in the first column have endings.
Write the same words without endings in the second column.

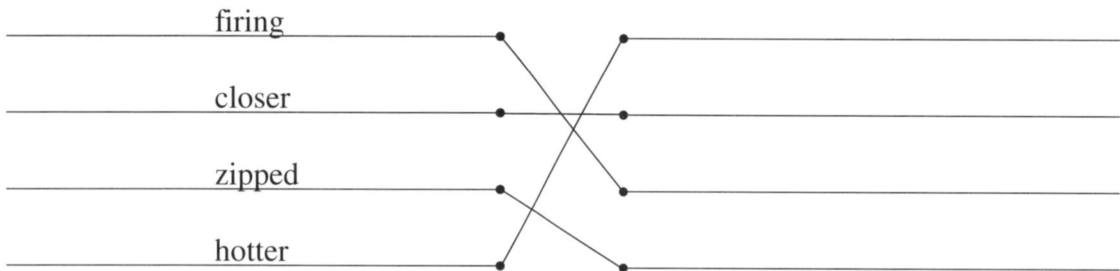

firing	
closer	
zipped	
hotter	

3 Write the word **louder.** Make a line over **loud.** ______________________________

Write the word **first.** Make a line under **ir.** ______________________________

 **4** Write the words.

may	+	be	=	
any	+	body	=	
near	+	ly	=	
her	+	self	=	

Individual Section

5 plop list gum dress tramp

stand crest pond fix must

5 Errors ______

6 smash when chips shop things

whisper there fresh wheels brush

6 Errors ______

7 dressed pinned spotted happened handed

dragged lifted zipped stepped slammed

7 Errors ______

8 trying plants bragging feels slaps

fastest slippery campers slowest teller

8 Errors ______

9 main please boards form bolt

painted beat grow older croak

could loud should mouth ouch

9 Errors ______

11

People were going in a ship from one land to another. They were sailing the sea when a bolt came out of the ship. And the ship began to sink. Men, women, and dogs were in the water. People were swimming and shouting. But the people and dogs were not sinking. They were holding on to boards. They yelled and yelled. One man did not yell. He whispered. This is what that man said, "I can't swim."

The other people grabbed on to him and kept him from sinking. Then a boat came by. A few people dragged him to the boat. When everybody was in the boat, they went to shore. They went faster and faster. They were saved.

11 Time ______   **12** Errors ______

13 *Record student's answers here:*

1. Why did the ship begin to sink?

   ____

2. Why did the people not sink?

   ____

3. What did the one man whisper? _______________________

4. How did the people help him?

   ____

5. Where did they go in the boat? _______________________

13 Errors ______

Decoding Strategies

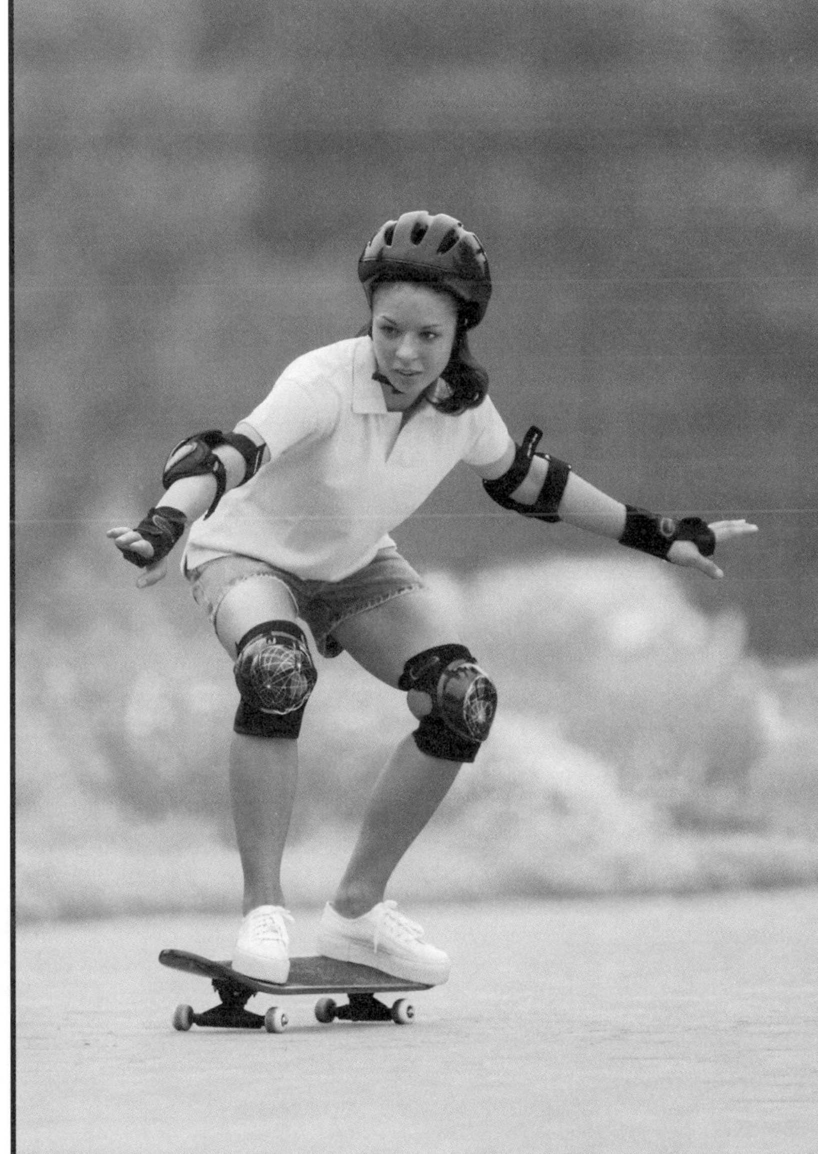

PHOTO CREDITS
Cover Photo: KS Studios

SRA/McGraw-Hill
A Division of The McGraw·Hill Companies

DECODING B1 MASTERY TEST 1
STUDENT PROFILE

Student _______________________   Teacher _______________________   Date _______________

<table>
<tr><td rowspan="2"></td><td rowspan="2">Skills tested</td><td>Number of errors</td><td>Pass criterion</td><td>Pass + Fail 0</td><td>If failed, review these lessons.</td></tr>
<tr><td></td><td></td><td></td><td></td></tr>
<tr><td rowspan="4">GROUP SECTION</td><td colspan="5">WORD IDENTIFICATION</td></tr>
<tr><td>1 Writing Letters for Sounds</td><td></td><td>Pass if 0–1 error</td><td></td><td>27–30</td></tr>
<tr><td>2 Writing Words without Endings</td><td></td><td>Pass if 0 errors</td><td></td><td>23, 25, 27, 29</td></tr>
<tr><td>3 Matching Completion</td><td></td><td>Pass if 0 errors</td><td></td><td>1–4</td></tr>
<tr><td>4 Sentence Copying</td><td></td><td>Pass if 0 errors</td><td></td><td>1–3</td></tr>
<tr><td rowspan="12">INDIVIDUAL SECTION</td><td>5 Short-Vowel Words</td><td></td><td>Pass if 0–1 error</td><td></td><td>1–9, 15, 16, 20, 25</td></tr>
<tr><td>6 Long-Vowel Words</td><td></td><td>Pass if 0–1 error</td><td></td><td>6, 8–10, 24–26</td></tr>
<tr><td>7 Sound Combinations</td><td></td><td>Pass if 0–1 error</td><td></td><td>1–9, 34, 35</td></tr>
<tr><td>8 Word Endings ed, ly, er</td><td></td><td>Pass if 0–1 error</td><td></td><td>23, 26, 28–35</td></tr>
<tr><td>9 Irregular Words</td><td></td><td>Pass if 0–1 error</td><td></td><td>27, 29–31</td></tr>
<tr><td colspan="2">STORY READING   Time</td><td></td><td></td><td></td></tr>
<tr><td>10 Rate (Time)</td><td></td><td>Pass if 80 secs. or less</td><td></td><td>28–35</td></tr>
<tr><td>11 Accuracy (Errors)</td><td></td><td>Pass if 0–4 errors</td><td></td><td>28–35</td></tr>
<tr><td>12 Comprehension</td><td></td><td>Pass if 0–1 error</td><td></td><td>28–35</td></tr>
</table>

TEST 1

2 The words in the first column have endings.
Write the same words without endings in the second column.

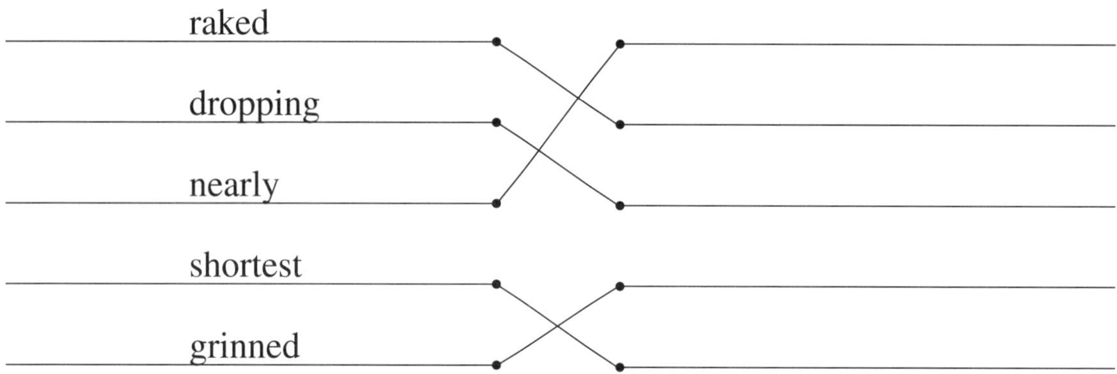

raked

dropping

nearly

shortest

grinned

3 Match the words and complete them.

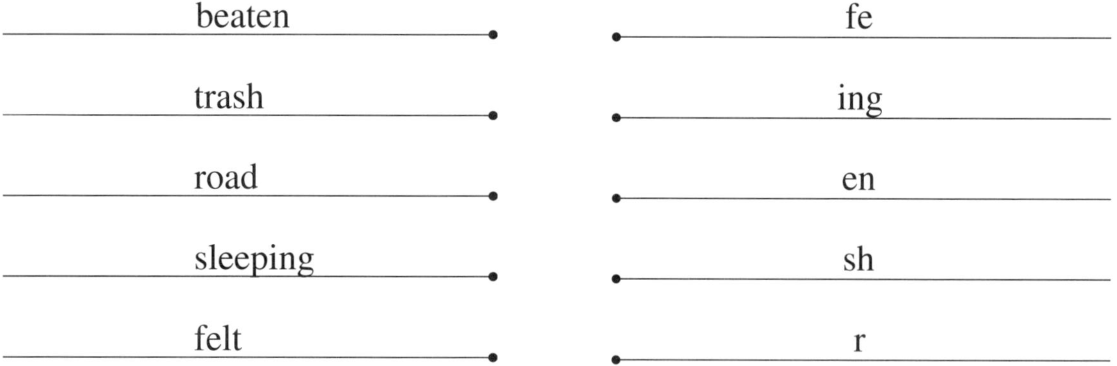

beaten   fe

trash   ing

road   en

sleeping   sh

felt   r

4 Copy this sentence:
The tramp gets in shape.

Individual Section

5 pack fell ramp win dug
not get bum pit drop

6 gate hope time week rider
nose fake wheel like shape

7 holds meal sore ranch load
reach horse board coldest heaps

8 sweeping hammer yearly grinned likely
stayed mopping handed popper bigger

8 Errors ______

9 minutes any people couldn't money

9 Errors ______

10

The tramp was getting in shape. When he got up, the sun was coming up over the hill in the east. When he went to bed, the sun was dropping in the west. He worked and worked every day. He sheared sheep. He made gates and pens for pigs. He dug holes for trees. He was getting thinner and thinner.

The tramp had stayed at the ranch for ten weeks. He told the rancher, "I need more meat and beans." "Yes," she said. "You have worked and worked. You are faster and thinner. You may have more meat and beans.

10 Time _____________   **11** Errors _______

12

Record student's answers here:

1. When did the tramp go to bed?

   ____

2. Name 2 things the tramp did for work at the ranch.

   ____

3. How long did the tramp stay at the ranch?

   ____

4. What did the tramp tell the rancher he needed?

   ____

5. Did the tramp get more to eat?

   ____

12 Errors _______

DECODING B1 MASTERY TEST 2
STUDENT PROFILE

Student _________________________ Teacher _________________________ Date _____________

	Skills tested		Number of errors	Pass criterion	Pass + Fail 0	If failed, review these lessons.
GROUP SECTION	**WORD IDENTIFICATION**					
	1 Identifying Letter Combinations			Pass if 0–1 error		40, 44, 45
	2 Writing Words without Endings			Pass if 0–1 error		52, 58–60
	3 Following Instructions			Pass if 0 errors		46, 47, 56
INDIVIDUAL SECTION	**4** Writing Compound Words			Pass if 0 errors		37–40, 42–45, 48, 62
	5 Short-Vowel Words			Pass if 0–1 error		49, 51–53, 59
	6 Consonant Digraphs			Pass if 0–1 error		9, 12, 47, 48, 52
	7 *ed* Endings in Short-Vowel Words			Pass if 0–1 error		13, 49, 58–61
	8 Word Endings *s, ing, est, er,* and *ery*			Pass if 0–1 error		27, 31, 45, 49, 63, 64
	9 Sound Combinations *ai, oa, or, ol, ea, ou, ow*			Pass if 0–2 errors		51, 52, 55, 61, 62
	10 Irregular Words			Pass if 0–1 error		50, 57–63
	STORY READING / **Time**					
	11 Rate (Time)			Pass if 80 secs. or less		61–65
	12 Accuracy (Errors)			Pass if 0–4 errors		61–65
	13 Comprehension			Pass if 0–1 error		61–65

TEST 2

1 Cross out the words that don't have **wh.**

where	with	that	when	how	wheel
word	then	what	why	week	who

2 The words in the first column have endings.
Write the same words without endings in the second column.

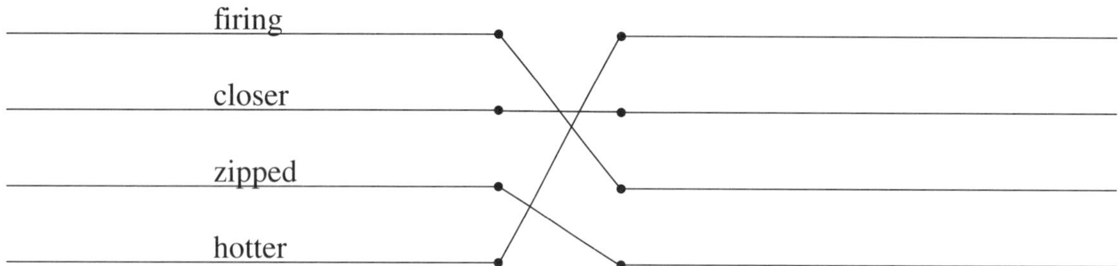

firing

closer

zipped

hotter

3 Write the word **louder.** Make a line over **loud.** ________________________

Write the word **first.** Make a line under **ir.** ________________________

4 Write the words.

___ may ___	+	___ be ___	=	________________
___ any ___	+	___ body ___	=	________________
___ near ___	+	___ ly ___	=	________________
___ her ___	+	___ self ___	=	________________

Individual Section

5 | plop | list | gum | dress | tramp
stand | crest | pond | fix | must

5 Errors _______

6 | smash | when | chips | shop | things
whisper | there | fresh | wheels | brush

6 Errors _______

7 | dressed | pinned | spotted | happened | handed
dragged | lifted | zipped | stepped | slammed

7 Errors _______

8 | trying | plants | bragging | feels | slaps
fastest | slippery | campers | slowest | teller

8 Errors _______

9 | main | please | boards | form | bolt
painted | beat | grow | older | croak
could | loud | should | mouth | ouch

9 Errors _______

10 together because private difference done

what millions brother know who

10 Errors _______

11

People were going in a ship from one land to another. They were sailing the sea when a bolt came out of the ship. And the ship began to sink. Men, women, and dogs were in the water. People were swimming and shouting. But the people and dogs were not sinking. They were holding on to boards. They yelled and yelled. One man did not yell. He whispered. This is what that man said, "I can't swim."

The other people grabbed on to him and kept him from sinking. Then a boat came by. A few people dragged him to the boat. When everybody was in the boat, they went to shore. They went faster and faster. They were saved.

11 Time _______________

12 Errors _______

13 *Record student's answers here:*

1. Why did the ship begin to sink?

   ____

2. Why did the people not sink?

   ____

3. What did the one man whisper? _______________________________________

4. How did the people help him?

   ____

5. Where did they go in the boat? _______________________________________

13 Errors _______

Decoding Strategies

Mastery Test Booklet
Decoding B1

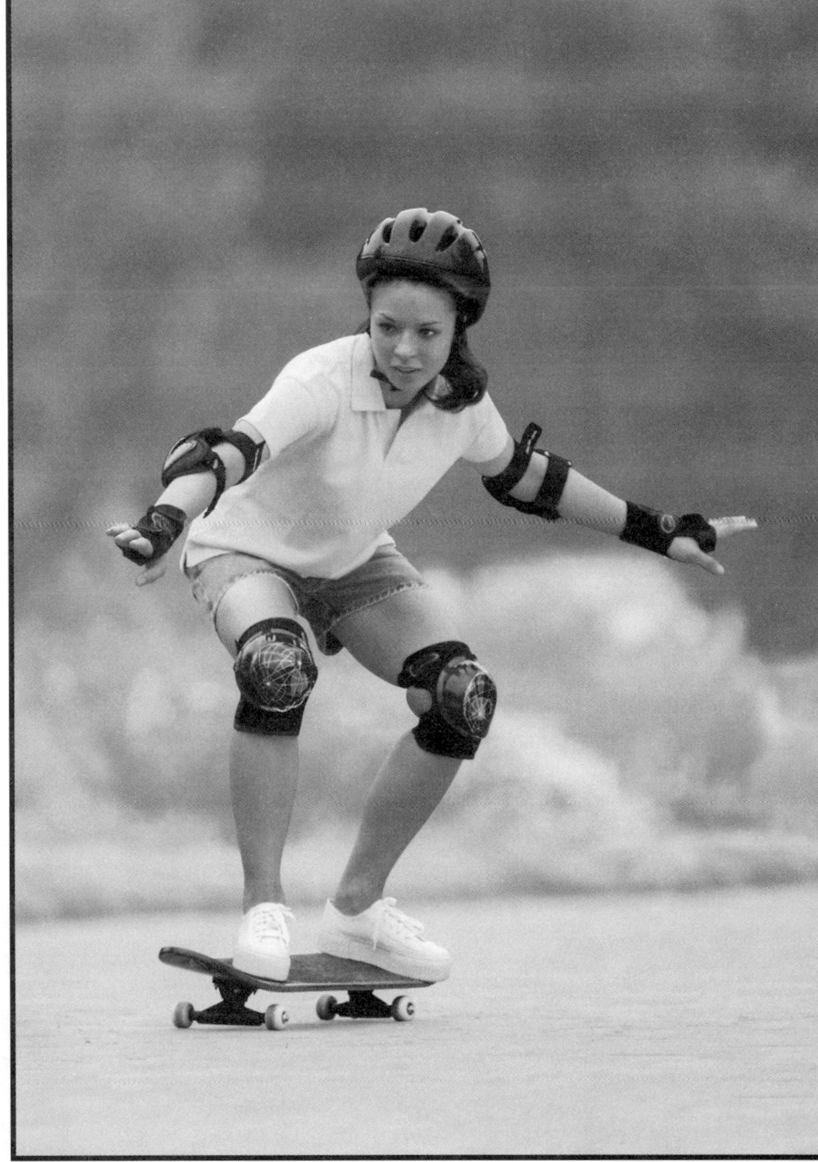

PHOTO CREDITS
Cover Photo: KS Studios

SRA/McGraw-Hill

A Division of The McGraw-Hill Companies

2002 Imprint
Copyright © 1999 by SRA/McGraw-Hill.

Send all inquiries to:
SRA/McGraw-Hill
8787 Orion Place
Columbus, Ohio 43240-4027

Printed in the United States of America.

R74782.01

13 14   MAZ 07 06 05 04

DECODING B1 MASTERY TEST 1
STUDENT PROFILE

Student ________________________ Teacher ________________________ Date ____________

	Skills tested	Number of errors	Pass criterion	Pass + Fail 0	If failed, review these lessons.
GROUP SECTION	**WORD IDENTIFICATION**				
	1 Writing Letters for Sounds		Pass if 0–1 error		27–30
	2 Writing Words without Endings		Pass if 0 errors		23, 25, 27, 29
	3 Matching Completion		Pass if 0 errors		1–4
	4 Sentence Copying		Pass if 0 errors		1–3
INDIVIDUAL SECTION	**5** Short-Vowel Words		Pass if 0–1 error		1–9, 15, 16, 20, 25
	6 Long-Vowel Words		Pass if 0–1 error		6, 8–10, 24–26
	7 Sound Combinations		Pass if 0–1 error		1–9, 34, 35
	8 Word Endings *ed, ly, er*		Pass if 0–1 error		23, 26, 28–35
	9 Irregular Words		Pass if 0–1 error		27, 29–31
	STORY READING — Time				
	10 Rate (Time)		Pass if 80 secs. or less		28–35
	11 Accuracy (Errors)		Pass if 0–4 errors		28–35
	12 Comprehension		Pass if 0–1 error		28–35

TEST 1

1

_______ _______ _______ _______ _______

_______ _______ _______ _______ _______

2 The words in the first column have endings.
Write the same words without endings in the second column.

raked

dropping

nearly

shortest

grinned

3 Match the words and complete them.

beaten   fe

trash   ing

road   en

sleeping   sh

felt   r

4 Copy this sentence:
The tramp gets in shape.

____

Individual Section

5 pack   fell   ramp   win   dug

    not   get   bum   pit   drop

5 Errors _______

6 gate   hope   time   week   rider

    nose   fake   wheel   like   shape

6 Errors _______

7 holds   meal   sore   ranch   load

    reach   horse   board   coldest   heaps

7 Errors _______

8 sweeping   hammer   yearly   grinned   likely

    stayed   mopping   handed   popper   bigger

8 Errors _______

9 minutes   any   people   couldn't   money

9 Errors _______

10

The tramp was getting in shape. When he got up, the sun was coming up over the hill in the east. When he went to bed, the sun was dropping in the west. He worked and worked every day. He sheared sheep. He made gates and pens for pigs. He dug holes for trees. He was getting thinner and thinner.

The tramp had stayed at the ranch for ten weeks. He told the rancher, "I need more meat and beans." "Yes," she said. "You have worked and worked. You are faster and thinner. You may have more meat and beans.

10 Time _____________   **11** Errors _______

12

Record student's answers here:

1. When did the tramp go to bed?

    ____

2. Name 2 things the tramp did for work at the ranch.

    ____

3. How long did the tramp stay at the ranch?

    ____

4. What did the tramp tell the rancher he needed?

    ____

5. Did the tramp get more to eat?

    ____

12 Errors _______

DECODING B1 MASTERY TEST 2
STUDENT PROFILE

Student ______________________   **Teacher** ______________________   **Date** ______________

	Skills tested		Number of errors	Pass criterion	Pass + Fail 0	If failed, review these lessons.
GROUP SECTION	**WORD IDENTIFICATION**					
	1	Identifying Letter Combinations		Pass if 0–1 error		40, 44, 45
	2	Writing Words without Endings		Pass if 0–1 error		52, 58–60
	3	Following Instructions		Pass if 0 errors		46, 47, 56
INDIVIDUAL SECTION	4	Writing Compound Words		Pass if 0 errors		37–40, 42–45, 48, 62
	5	Short-Vowel Words		Pass if 0–1 error		49, 51–53, 59
	6	Consonant Digraphs		Pass if 0–1 error		9, 12, 47, 48, 52
	7	*ed* Endings in Short-Vowel Words		Pass if 0–1 error		13, 49, 58–61
	8	Word Endings *s, ing, est, er,* and *ery*		Pass if 0–1 error		27, 31, 45, 49, 63, 64
	9	Sound Combinations *ai, oa, or, ol, ea, ou, ow*		Pass if 0–2 errors		51, 52, 55, 61, 62
	10	Irregular Words		Pass if 0–1 error		50, 57–63
	STORY READING	**Time**				
	11	Rate (Time)		Pass if 80 secs. or less		61–65
	12	Accuracy (Errors)		Pass if 0–4 errors		61–65
	13	Comprehension		Pass if 0–1 error		61–65

TEST 2

 Cross out the words that don't have **wh.**

where   with   that   when   how   wheel

word   then   what   why   week   who

 The words in the first column have endings.
Write the same words without endings in the second column.

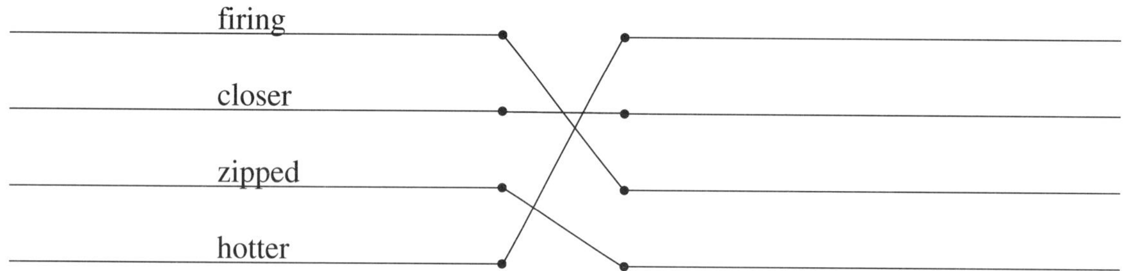

firing

closer

zipped

hotter

 Write the word **louder.** Make a line over **loud.** _______________________

Write the word **first.** Make a line under **ir.** _______________________

Write the words.

_____ may _____ + _____ be _____ = _______________________

_____ any _____ + _____ body _____ = _______________________

_____ near _____ + _____ ly _____ = _______________________

_____ her _____ + _____ self _____ = _______________________

Individual Section

5 plop list gum dress tramp

stand crest pond fix must

5 Errors _______

6 smash when chips shop things

whisper there fresh wheels brush

6 Errors _______

7 dressed pinned spotted happened handed

dragged lifted zipped stepped slammed

7 Errors _______

8 trying plants bragging feels slaps

fastest slippery campers slowest teller

8 Errors _______

9 main please boards form bolt

painted beat grow older croak

could loud should mouth ouch

9 Errors _______

10 together   because   private   difference   done

what   millions   brother   know   who

10 Errors _______

11

People were going in a ship from one land to another. They were sailing the sea when a bolt came out of the ship. And the ship began to sink. Men, women, and dogs were in the water. People were swimming and shouting. But the people and dogs were not sinking. They were holding on to boards. They yelled and yelled. One man did not yell. He whispered. This is what that man said, "I can't swim."

The other people grabbed on to him and kept him from sinking. Then a boat came by. A few people dragged him to the boat. When everybody was in the boat, they went to shore. They went faster and faster. They were saved.

11 Time ______________

12 Errors _______

13 *Record student's answers here:*

1. Why did the ship begin to sink?

____

2. Why did the people not sink?

____

3. What did the one man whisper? _______________________________

4. How did the people help him?

____

5. Where did they go in the boat? ______________________________

13 Errors _______

Decoding Strategies

Mastery Test Booklet
Decoding B1

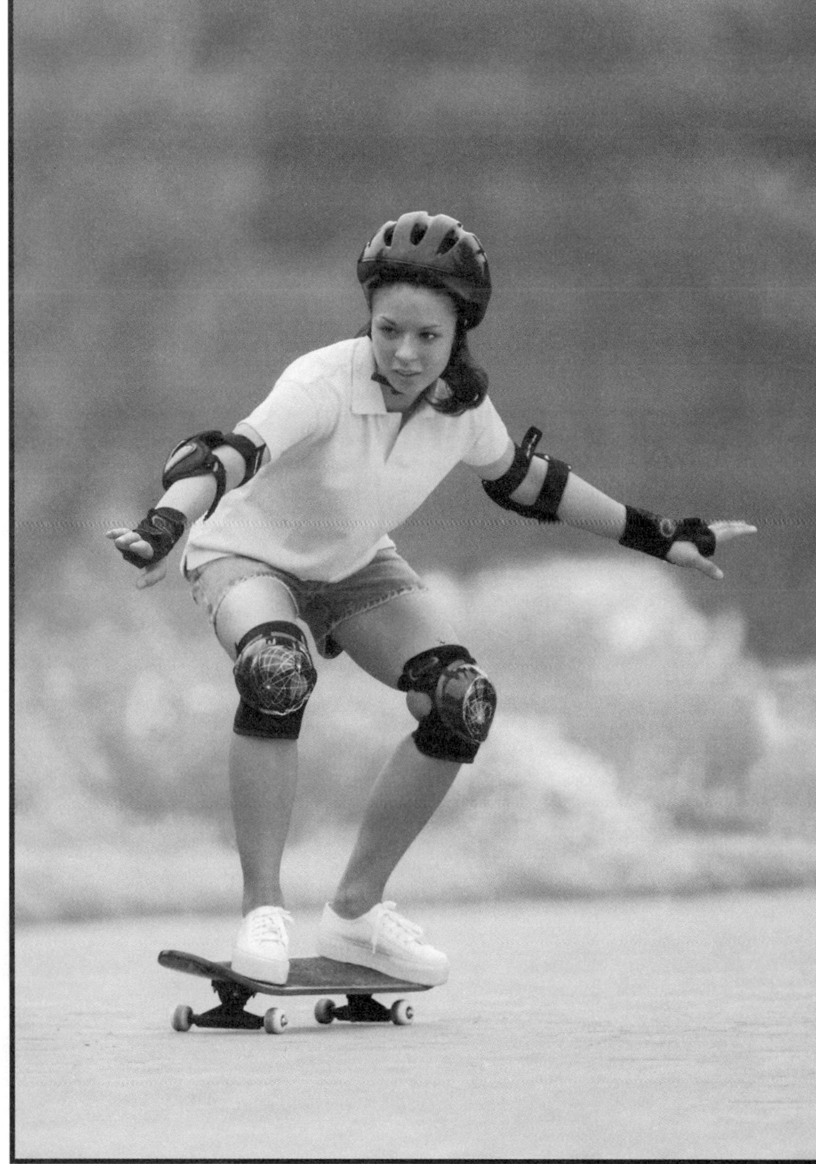

PHOTO CREDITS
Cover Photo: KS Studios

SRA/McGraw-Hill

A Division of The McGraw-Hill Companies

2002 Imprint
Copyright © 1999 by SRA/McGraw-Hill.

Send all inquiries to:
SRA/McGraw-Hill
8787 Orion Place
Columbus, Ohio 43240-4027

Printed in the United States of America.

R74782.01

13 14   MAZ 07 06 05 04

DECODING B1 MASTERY TEST 1
STUDENT PROFILE

Student _________________________   Teacher _________________________   Date _____________

	Skills tested	Number of errors	Pass criterion	Pass + Fail 0	If failed, review these lessons.
GROUP SECTION	**WORD IDENTIFICATION**				
	1 Writing Letters for Sounds		Pass if 0–1 error		27–30
	2 Writing Words without Endings		Pass if 0 errors		23, 25, 27, 29
	3 Matching Completion		Pass if 0 errors		1–4
	4 Sentence Copying		Pass if 0 errors		1–3
INDIVIDUAL SECTION	**5** Short-Vowel Words		Pass if 0–1 error		1–9, 15, 16, 20, 25
	6 Long-Vowel Words		Pass if 0–1 error		6, 8–10, 24–26
	7 Sound Combinations		Pass if 0–1 error		1–9, 34, 35
	8 Word Endings *ed, ly, er*		Pass if 0–1 error		23, 26, 28–35
	9 Irregular Words		Pass if 0–1 error		27, 29–31
	STORY READING Time				
	10 Rate (Time)		Pass if 80 secs. or less		28–35
	11 Accuracy (Errors)		Pass if 0–4 errors		28–35
	12 Comprehension		Pass if 0–1 error		28–35

TEST 1

1

_____________   _____________   _____________   _____________

_____________   _____________   _____________   _____________

2 The words in the first column have endings.
Write the same words without endings in the second column.

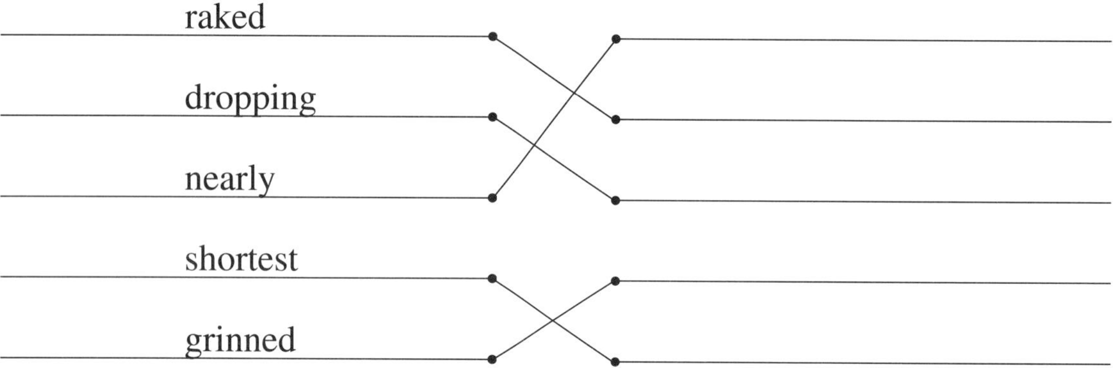

raked

dropping

nearly

shortest

grinned

3 Match the words and complete them.

beaten   fe

trash   ing

road   en

sleeping   sh

felt   r

4 Copy this sentence:
The tramp gets in shape.

____

Individual Section

5
| pack | fell | ramp | win | dug |
| not | get | bum | pit | drop |

5 Errors ______

6
| gate | hope | time | week | rider |
| nose | fake | wheel | like | shape |

6 Errors ______

7
| holds | meal | sore | ranch | load |
| reach | horse | board | coldest | heaps |

7 Errors ______

8
| sweeping | hammer | yearly | grinned | likely |
| stayed | mopping | handed | popper | bigger |

8 Errors ______

9
| minutes | any | people | couldn't | money |

9 Errors ______

The tramp was getting in shape. When he got up, the sun was coming up over the hill in the east. When he went to bed, the sun was dropping in the west. He worked and worked every day. He sheared sheep. He made gates and pens for pigs. He dug holes for trees. He was getting thinner and thinner.

The tramp had stayed at the ranch for ten weeks. He told the rancher, "I need more meat and beans." "Yes," she said. "You have worked and worked. You are faster and thinner. You may have more meat and beans.

10 Time _______________   **11** Errors _______

12

Record student's answers here:

1. When did the tramp go to bed?

____

2. Name 2 things the tramp did for work at the ranch.

____

3. How long did the tramp stay at the ranch?

____

4. What did the tramp tell the rancher he needed?

____

5. Did the tramp get more to eat?

____

12 Errors _______

Student ______________________ Teacher ______________________ Date ______________

	Skills tested		Number of errors	Pass criterion	Pass + Fail 0	If failed, review these lessons.
GROUP SECTION	**WORD IDENTIFICATION**					
	1	Identifying Letter Combinations		Pass if 0–1 error		40, 44, 45
	2	Writing Words without Endings		Pass if 0–1 error		52, 58–60
	3	Following Instructions		Pass if 0 errors		46, 47, 56
INDIVIDUAL SECTION	**4**	Writing Compound Words		Pass if 0 errors		37–40, 42–45, 48, 62
	5	Short-Vowel Words		Pass if 0–1 error		49, 51–53, 59
	6	Consonant Digraphs		Pass if 0–1 error		9, 12, 47, 48, 52
	7	*ed* Endings in Short-Vowel Words		Pass if 0–1 error		13, 49, 58–61
	8	Word Endings *s, ing, est, er,* and *ery*		Pass if 0–1 error		27, 31, 45, 49, 63, 64
	9	Sound Combinations *ai, oa, or, ol, ea, ou, ow*		Pass if 0–2 errors		51, 52, 55, 61, 62
	10	Irregular Words		Pass if 0–1 error		50, 57–63
	STORY READING	**Time**				
	11	Rate (Time)			Pass if 80 secs. or less		61–65
	12	Accuracy (Errors)			Pass if 0–4 errors		61–65
	13	Comprehension		Pass if 0–1 error		61–65

TEST 2

 Cross out the words that don't have **wh.**

where   with   that   when   how   wheel

word   then   what   why   week   who

 The words in the first column have endings.
Write the same words without endings in the second column.

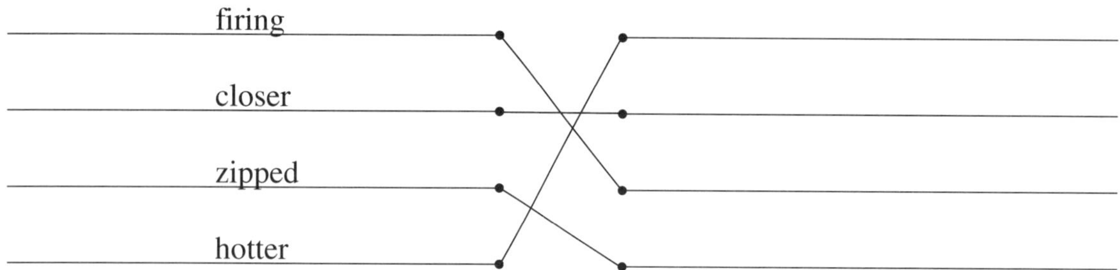

firing

closer

zipped

hotter

Write the word **louder.** Make a line over **loud.** ________________________

Write the word **first.** Make a line under **ir.** ________________________

 Write the words.

may	+	be	=	
any	+	body	=	
near	+	ly	=	
her	+	self	=	

Individual Section

5 plop list gum dress tramp

stand crest pond fix must

5 **Errors** _____

6 smash when chips shop things

whisper there fresh wheels brush

6 **Errors** _____

7 dressed pinned spotted happened handed

dragged lifted zipped stepped slammed

7 **Errors** _____

8 trying plants bragging feels slaps

fastest slippery campers slowest teller

8 **Errors** _____

9 main please boards form bolt

painted beat grow older croak

could loud should mouth ouch

9 **Errors** _____

together	because	private	difference	done
what	millions	brother	know	who

10 Errors _______

11

People were going in a ship from one land to another. They were sailing the sea when a bolt came out of the ship. And the ship began to sink. Men, women, and dogs were in the water. People were swimming and shouting. But the people and dogs were not sinking. They were holding on to boards. They yelled and yelled. One man did not yell. He whispered. This is what that man said, "I can't swim."

The other people grabbed on to him and kept him from sinking. Then a boat came by. A few people dragged him to the boat. When everybody was in the boat, they went to shore. They went faster and faster. They were saved.

11 Time _______________   **12** Errors _______

13 *Record student's answers here:*

1. Why did the ship begin to sink?

    ____

2. Why did the people not sink?

    ____

3. What did the one man whisper? _______________________

4. How did the people help him?

    ____

5. Where did they go in the boat? _______________________

13 Errors _______

Decoding Strategies

Mastery Test Booklet
Decoding B1

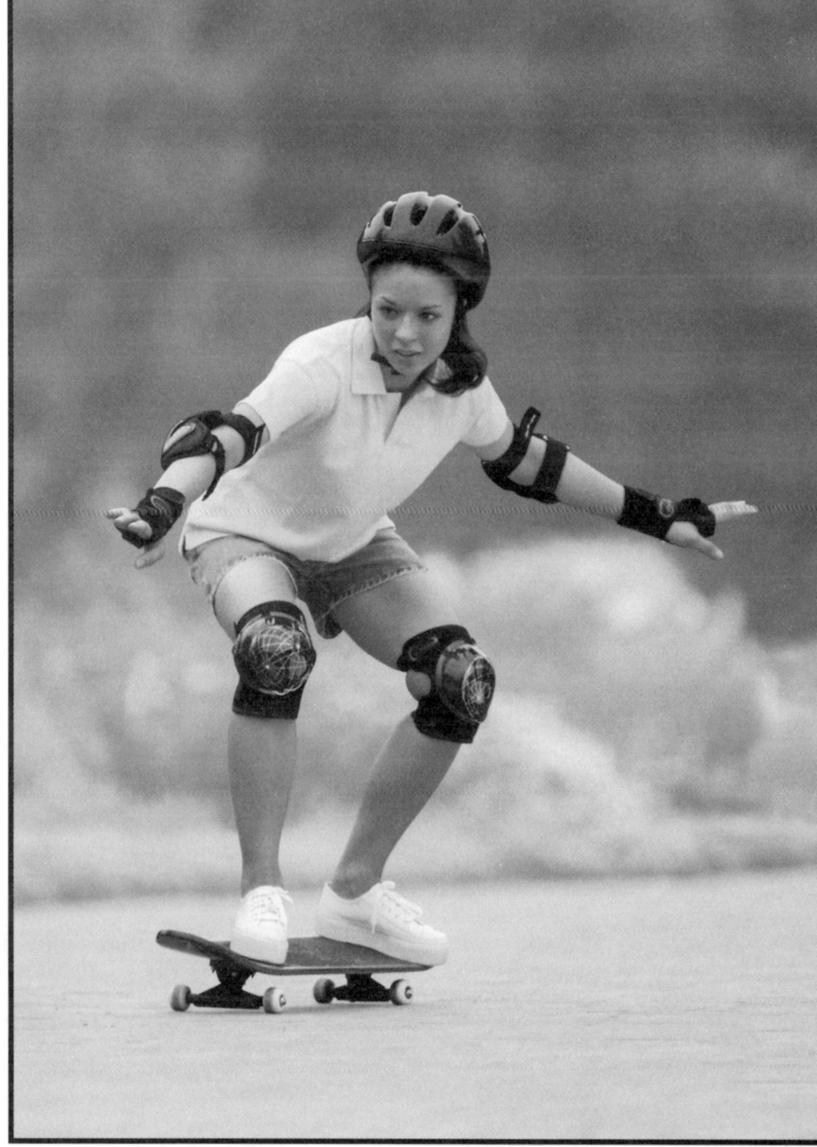

PHOTO CREDITS
Cover Photo: KS Studios

SRA/McGraw-Hill

*A Division of The **McGraw·Hill** Companies*

2002 Imprint
Copyright © 1999 by SRA/McGraw-Hill.

Send all inquiries to:
SRA/McGraw-Hill
8787 Orion Place
Columbus, Ohio 43240-4027

Printed in the United States of America.

R74782.01

    13 14   MAZ 07 06 05 04

Student _________________________   Teacher _________________________   Date _______________

<table>
<tr><td rowspan="2"></td><td rowspan="2">Skills tested</td><td colspan="2">Number of errors</td><td>Pass criterion</td><td>Pass + Fail 0</td><td>If failed, review these lessons.</td></tr>
<tr><td colspan="2"></td><td></td><td></td><td></td></tr>
<tr><td rowspan="4">GROUP SECTION</td><td colspan="6">WORD IDENTIFICATION</td></tr>
<tr><td>1   Writing Letters for Sounds</td><td colspan="2"></td><td>Pass if 0–1 error</td><td></td><td>27–30</td></tr>
<tr><td>2   Writing Words without Endings</td><td colspan="2"></td><td>Pass if 0 errors</td><td></td><td>23, 25, 27, 29</td></tr>
<tr><td>3   Matching Completion</td><td colspan="2"></td><td>Pass if 0 errors</td><td></td><td>1–4</td></tr>
<tr><td rowspan="9">INDIVIDUAL SECTION</td><td>4   Sentence Copying</td><td colspan="2"></td><td>Pass if 0 errors</td><td></td><td>1–3</td></tr>
<tr><td>5   Short-Vowel Words</td><td colspan="2"></td><td>Pass if 0–1 error</td><td></td><td>1–9, 15, 16, 20, 25</td></tr>
<tr><td>6   Long-Vowel Words</td><td colspan="2"></td><td>Pass if 0–1 error</td><td></td><td>6, 8–10, 24–26</td></tr>
<tr><td>7   Sound Combinations</td><td colspan="2"></td><td>Pass if 0–1 error</td><td></td><td>1–9, 34, 35</td></tr>
<tr><td>8   Word Endings ed, ly, er</td><td colspan="2"></td><td>Pass if 0–1 error</td><td></td><td>23, 26, 28–35</td></tr>
<tr><td>9   Irregular Words</td><td colspan="2"></td><td>Pass if 0–1 error</td><td></td><td>27, 29–31</td></tr>
<tr><td colspan="2">STORY READING   Time</td><td></td><td></td><td></td></tr>
<tr><td>10   Rate (Time)</td><td></td><td></td><td>Pass if 80 secs. or less</td><td></td><td>28–35</td></tr>
<tr><td>11   Accuracy (Errors)</td><td></td><td></td><td>Pass if 0–4 errors</td><td></td><td>28–35</td></tr>
<tr><td rowspan="1"></td><td>12   Comprehension</td><td colspan="2"></td><td>Pass if 0–1 error</td><td></td><td>28–35</td></tr>
</table>

TEST 1

NAME ___________________

1

___________ ___________ ___________ ___________ ___________

___________ ___________ ___________ ___________ ___________

2 The words in the first column have endings.
Write the same words without endings in the second column.

raked

dropping

nearly

shortest

grinned

3 Match the words and complete them.

beaten   fe

trash   ing

road   en

sleeping   sh

felt   r

4 Copy this sentence:
The tramp gets in shape.

____

Individual Section

5   pack   fell   ramp   win   dug

     not   get   bum   pit   drop

6   gate   hope   time   week   rider

     nose   fake   wheel   like   shape

7   holds   meal   sore   ranch   load

     reach   horse   board   coldest   heaps

8   sweeping   hammer   yearly   grinned   likely

     stayed   mopping   handed   popper   bigger

8 Errors ______

9   minutes   any   people   couldn't   money

9 Errors ______

10

The tramp was getting in shape. When he got up, the sun was coming up over the hill in the east. When he went to bed, the sun was dropping in the west. He worked and worked every day. He sheared sheep. He made gates and pens for pigs. He dug holes for trees. He was getting thinner and thinner.

The tramp had stayed at the ranch for ten weeks. He told the rancher, "I need more meat and beans." "Yes," she said. "You have worked and worked. You are faster and thinner. You may have more meat and beans.

10 Time _____________   **11** Errors _______

12

Record student's answers here:

1. When did the tramp go to bed?

   ____

2. Name 2 things the tramp did for work at the ranch.

   ____

3. How long did the tramp stay at the ranch?

   ____

4. What did the tramp tell the rancher he needed?

   ____

5. Did the tramp get more to eat?

   ____

12 Errors _______

DECODING B1 MASTERY TEST 2
STUDENT PROFILE

Student ______________________ Teacher ______________________ Date ______________

	Skills tested		Number of errors	Pass criterion	Pass + Fail 0	If failed, review these lessons.
GROUP SECTION	**WORD IDENTIFICATION**					
	1	Identifying Letter Combinations		Pass if 0–1 error		40, 44, 45
	2	Writing Words without Endings		Pass if 0–1 error		52, 58–60
	3	Following Instructions		Pass if 0 errors		46, 47, 56
INDIVIDUAL SECTION	4	Writing Compound Words		Pass if 0 errors		37–40, 42–45, 48, 62
	5	Short-Vowel Words		Pass if 0–1 error		49, 51–53, 59
	6	Consonant Digraphs		Pass if 0–1 error		9, 12, 47, 48, 52
	7	*ed* Endings in Short-Vowel Words		Pass if 0–1 error		13, 49, 58–61
	8	Word Endings *s, ing, est, er,* and *ery*		Pass if 0–1 error		27, 31, 45, 49, 63, 64
	9	Sound Combinations *ai, oa, or, ol, ea, ou, ow*		Pass if 0–2 errors		51, 52, 55, 61, 62
	10	Irregular Words		Pass if 0–1 error		50, 57–63
	STORY READING	**Time**				
	11	Rate (Time)		Pass if 80 secs. or less		61–65
	12	Accuracy (Errors)		Pass if 0–4 errors		61–65
	13	Comprehension		Pass if 0–1 error		61–65

TEST 2

NAME _________________________________

 **1** Cross out the words that don't have **wh.**

where   with   that   when   how   wheel

word   then   what   why   week   who

 **2** The words in the first column have endings.
Write the same words without endings in the second column.

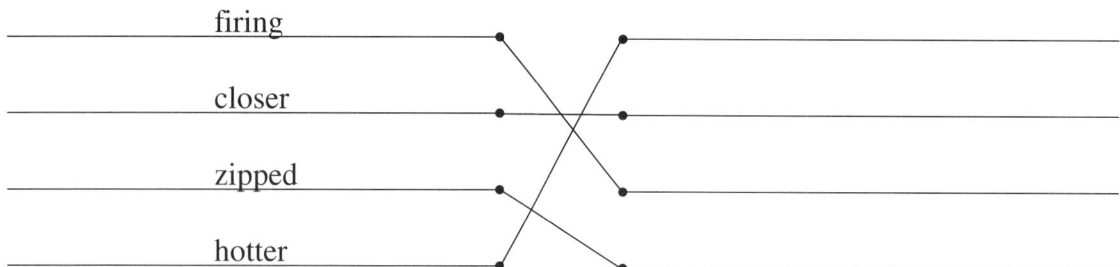

3 Write the word **louder.** Make a line over **loud.** ________________________

Write the word **first.** Make a line under **ir.** ________________________

4 Write the words.

may	+ be	=
any	+ body	=
near	+ ly	=
her	+ self	=

Individual Section

| **5** | plop | list | gum | dress | tramp | | **5** Errors _____ |
| | stand | crest | pond | fix | must | | |

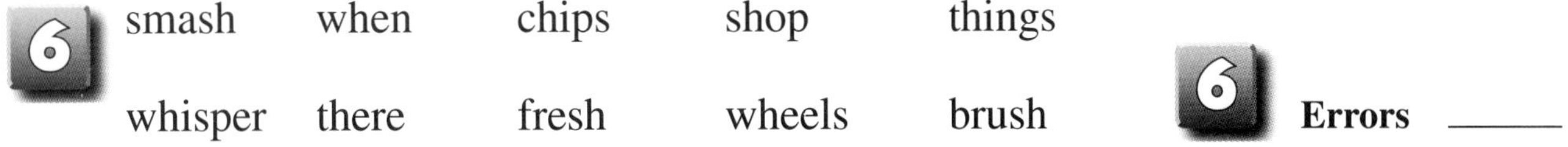

| **6** | smash | when | chips | shop | things | | **6** Errors _____ |
| | whisper | there | fresh | wheels | brush | | |

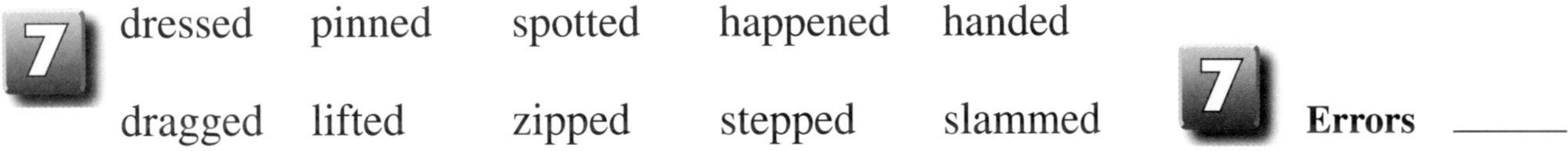

| **7** | dressed | pinned | spotted | happened | handed | | **7** Errors _____ |
| | dragged | lifted | zipped | stepped | slammed | | |

| **8** | trying | plants | bragging | feels | slaps | | **8** Errors _____ |
| | fastest | slippery | campers | slowest | teller | | |

9	main	please	boards	form	bolt		**9** Errors _____
	painted	beat	grow	older	croak		
	could	loud	should	mouth	ouch		

10

10 together   because   private   difference   done

what   millions   brother   know   who

10 Errors _______

11

People were going in a ship from one land to another. They were sailing the sea when a bolt came out of the ship. And the ship began to sink. Men, women, and dogs were in the water. People were swimming and shouting. But the people and dogs were not sinking. They were holding on to boards. They yelled and yelled. One man did not yell. He whispered. This is what that man said, "I can't swim."

The other people grabbed on to him and kept him from sinking. Then a boat came by. A few people dragged him to the boat. When everybody was in the boat, they went to shore. They went faster and faster. They were saved.

11 Time _______________   **12** Errors _______

13 *Record student's answers here:*

1. Why did the ship begin to sink?

____

2. Why did the people not sink?

____

3. What did the one man whisper?   _______________________________

4. How did the people help him?

____

5. Where did they go in the boat?   _______________________________

13 Errors _______

Decoding Strategies

Mastery Test Booklet
Decoding B1

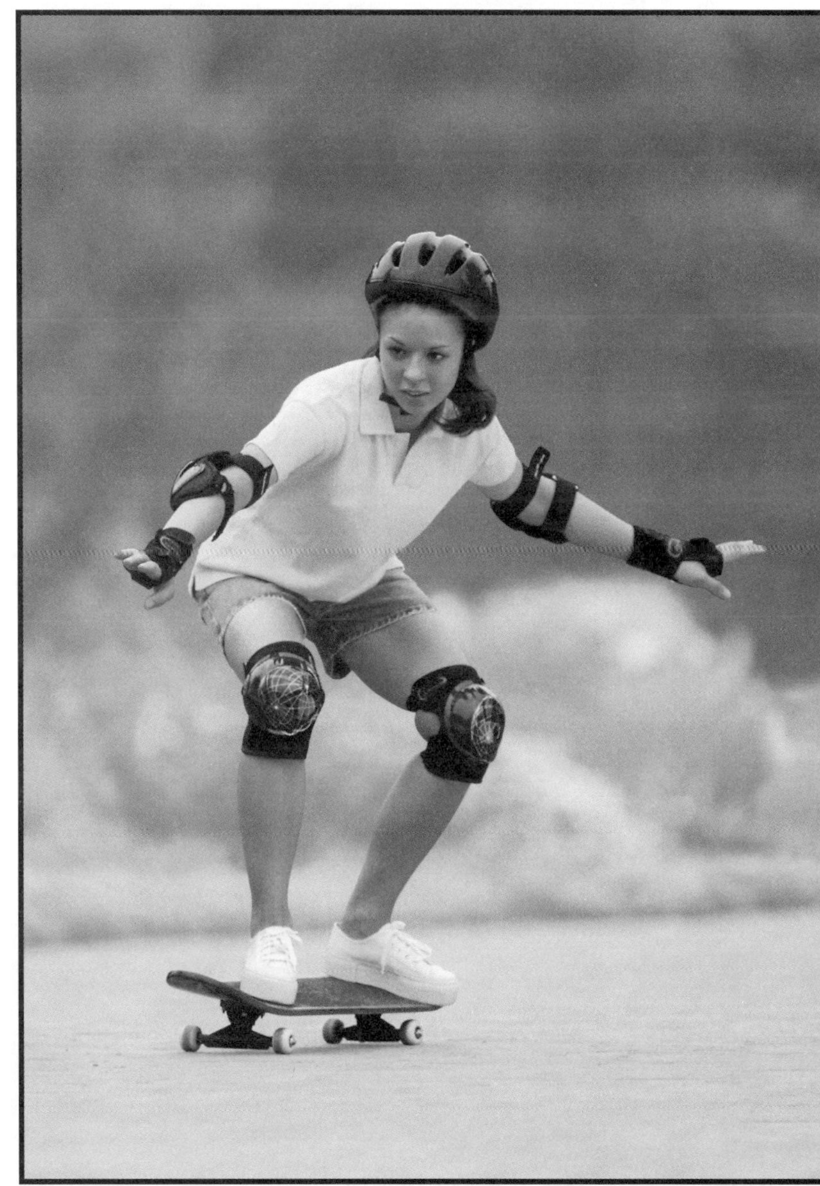

PHOTO CREDITS
Cover Photo: KS Studios

SRA/McGraw-Hill

A Division of The McGraw·Hill Companies

2002 Imprint
Copyright © 1999 by SRA/McGraw-Hill.

Send all inquiries to:
SRA/McGraw-Hill
8787 Orion Place
Columbus, Ohio 43240-4027

Printed in the United States of America.

R74782.01

13 14   MAZ 07 06 05 04

DECODING B1 MASTERY TEST 1
STUDENT PROFILE

Student ______________________ Teacher ______________________ Date ______________

	Skills tested		Number of errors	Pass criterion	Pass + Fail 0	If failed, review these lessons.
GROUP SECTION		**WORD IDENTIFICATION**				
	1	Writing Letters for Sounds		Pass if 0–1 error		27–30
	2	Writing Words without Endings		Pass if 0 errors		23, 25, 27, 29
	3	Matching Completion		Pass if 0 errors		1–4
	4	Sentence Copying		Pass if 0 errors		1–3
INDIVIDUAL SECTION	**5**	Short-Vowel Words		Pass if 0–1 error		1–9, 15, 16, 20, 25
	6	Long-Vowel Words		Pass if 0–1 error		6, 8–10, 24–26
	7	Sound Combinations		Pass if 0–1 error		1–9, 34, 35
	8	Word Endings *ed, ly, er*		Pass if 0–1 error		23, 26, 28–35
	9	Irregular Words		Pass if 0–1 error		27, 29–31
		STORY READING / **Time**				
	10	Rate (Time)		Pass if 80 secs. or less		28–35
	11	Accuracy (Errors)		Pass if 0–4 errors		28–35
	12	Comprehension		Pass if 0–1 error		28–35

NAME _______________________

1

___________ ___________ ___________ ___________

___________ ___________ ___________ ___________

2 The words in the first column have endings.
Write the same words without endings in the second column.

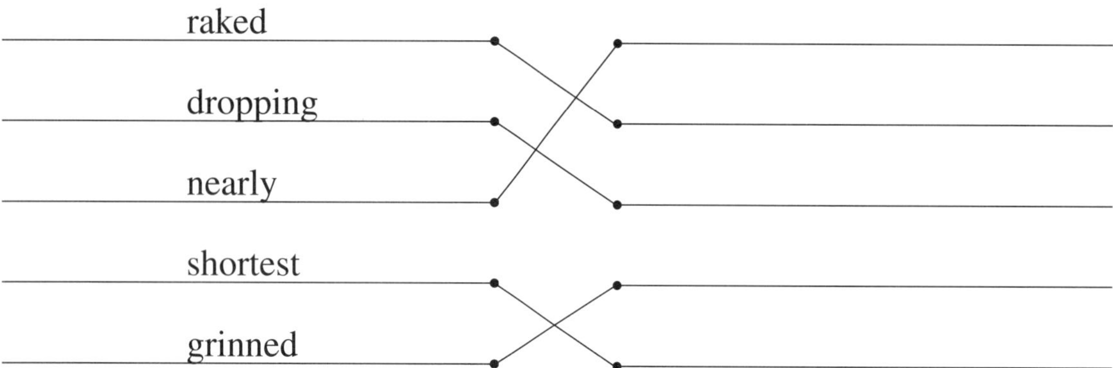

raked	
dropping	
nearly	
shortest	
grinned	

3 Match the words and complete them.

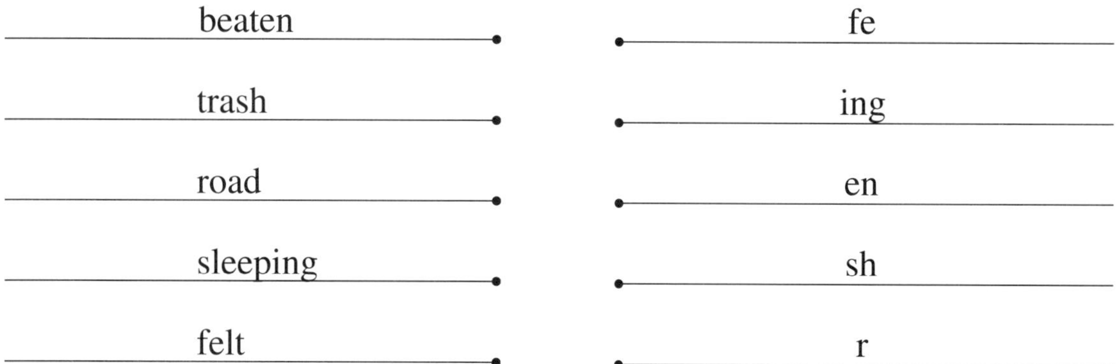

beaten	fe
trash	ing
road	en
sleeping	sh
felt	r

4 Copy this sentence:
The tramp gets in shape.

____

Individual Section

5   pack   fell   ramp   win   dug

not   get   bum   pit   drop

5   Errors _______

6   gate   hope   time   week   rider

nose   fake   wheel   like   shape

6   Errors _______

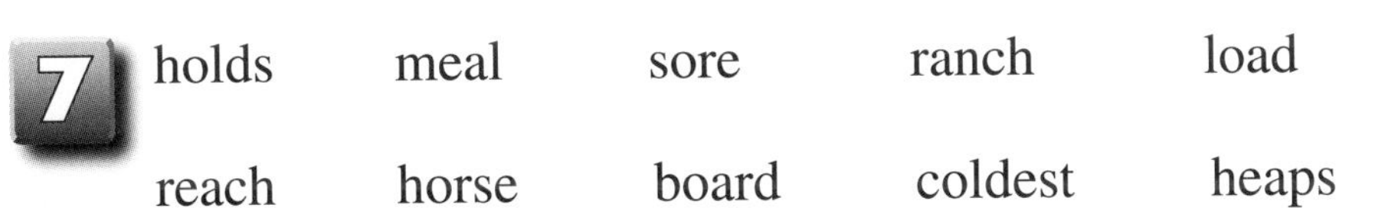

7   holds   meal   sore   ranch   load

reach   horse   board   coldest   heaps

7   Errors _______

8   sweeping   hammer   yearly   grinned   likely

stayed   mopping   handed   popper   bigger

8   Errors _______

9   minutes   any   people   couldn't   money

9   Errors _______

10

The tramp was getting in shape. When he got up, the sun was coming up over the hill in the east. When he went to bed, the sun was dropping in the west. He worked and worked every day. He sheared sheep. He made gates and pens for pigs. He dug holes for trees. He was getting thinner and thinner.

The tramp had stayed at the ranch for ten weeks. He told the rancher, "I need more meat and beans." "Yes," she said. "You have worked and worked. You are faster and thinner. You may have more meat and beans.

10 Time —————— **11** Errors ———

12

Record student's answers here:

1. When did the tramp go to bed?

   ____

2. Name 2 things the tramp did for work at the ranch.

   ____

3. How long did the tramp stay at the ranch?

   ____

4. What did the tramp tell the rancher he needed?

   ____

5. Did the tramp get more to eat?

   ____

12 Errors ———

DECODING B1 MASTERY TEST 2
STUDENT PROFILE

Student _______________________ Teacher _______________________ Date _______________

	Skills tested	Number of errors	Pass criterion	Pass + Fail 0	If failed, review these lessons.
GROUP SECTION	**WORD IDENTIFICATION**				
	1 Identifying Letter Combinations		Pass if 0–1 error		40, 44, 45
	2 Writing Words without Endings		Pass if 0–1 error		52, 58–60
	3 Following Instructions		Pass if 0 errors		46, 47, 56
INDIVIDUAL SECTION	4 Writing Compound Words		Pass if 0 errors		37–40, 42–45, 48, 62
	5 Short-Vowel Words		Pass if 0–1 error		49, 51–53, 59
	6 Consonant Digraphs		Pass if 0–1 error		9, 12, 47, 48, 52
	7 *ed* Endings in Short-Vowel Words		Pass if 0–1 error		13, 49, 58–61
	8 Word Endings *s, ing, est, er,* and *ery*		Pass if 0–1 error		27, 31, 45, 49, 63, 64
	9 Sound Combinations *ai, oa, or, ol, ea, ou, ow*		Pass if 0–2 errors		51, 52, 55, 61, 62
	10 Irregular Words		Pass if 0–1 error		50, 57–63
	STORY READING / Time				
	11 Rate (Time)		Pass if 80 secs. or less		61–65
	12 Accuracy (Errors)		Pass if 0–4 errors		61–65
	13 Comprehension		Pass if 0–1 error		61–65

 # TEST 2

NAME _______________________________

Cross out the words that don't have wh.

where	with	that	when	how	wheel
word	then	what	why	week	who

**The words in the first column have endings.
Write the same words without endings in the second column.**

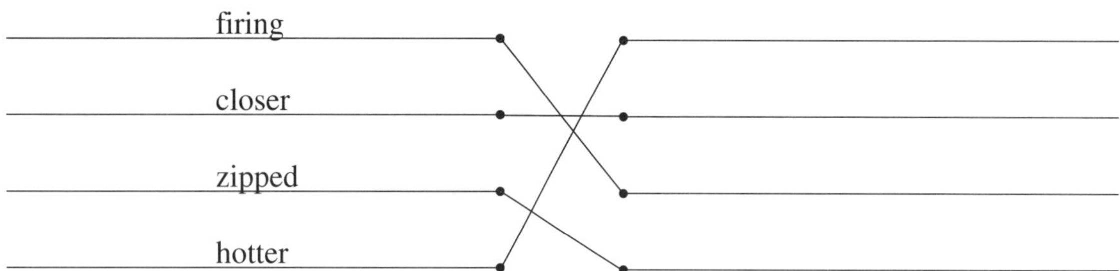

firing

closer

zipped

hotter

Write the word louder. Make a line over loud. _______________________________

Write the word first. Make a line under ir. _______________________________

Write the words.

may	+	be	=	
any	+	body	=	
near	+	ly	=	
her	+	self	=	

Individual Section

5 plop   list   gum   dress   tramp

stand   crest   pond   fix   must

5 Errors _______

6 smash   when   chips   shop   things

whisper   there   fresh   wheels   brush

6 Errors _______

7 dressed   pinned   spotted   happened   handed

dragged   lifted   zipped   stepped   slammed

7 Errors _______

8 trying   plants   bragging   feels   slaps

fastest   slippery   campers   slowest   teller

8 Errors _______

9 main   please   boards   form   bolt

painted   beat   grow   older   croak

could   loud   should   mouth   ouch

9 Errors _______

11

People were going in a ship from one land to another. They were sailing the sea when a bolt came out of the ship. And the ship began to sink. Men, women, and dogs were in the water. People were swimming and shouting. But the people and dogs were not sinking. They were holding on to boards. They yelled and yelled. One man did not yell. He whispered. This is what that man said, "I can't swim."

The other people grabbed on to him and kept him from sinking. Then a boat came by. A few people dragged him to the boat. When everybody was in the boat, they went to shore. They went faster and faster. They were saved.

11 Time ____________   **12** Errors ______

13 *Record student's answers here:*

1. Why did the ship begin to sink?

   ____

2. Why did the people not sink?

   ____

3. What did the one man whisper? ________________________________

4. How did the people help him?

   ____

5. Where did they go in the boat? ________________________________

13 Errors ______

Decoding Strategies

Mastery Test Booklet
Decoding B1

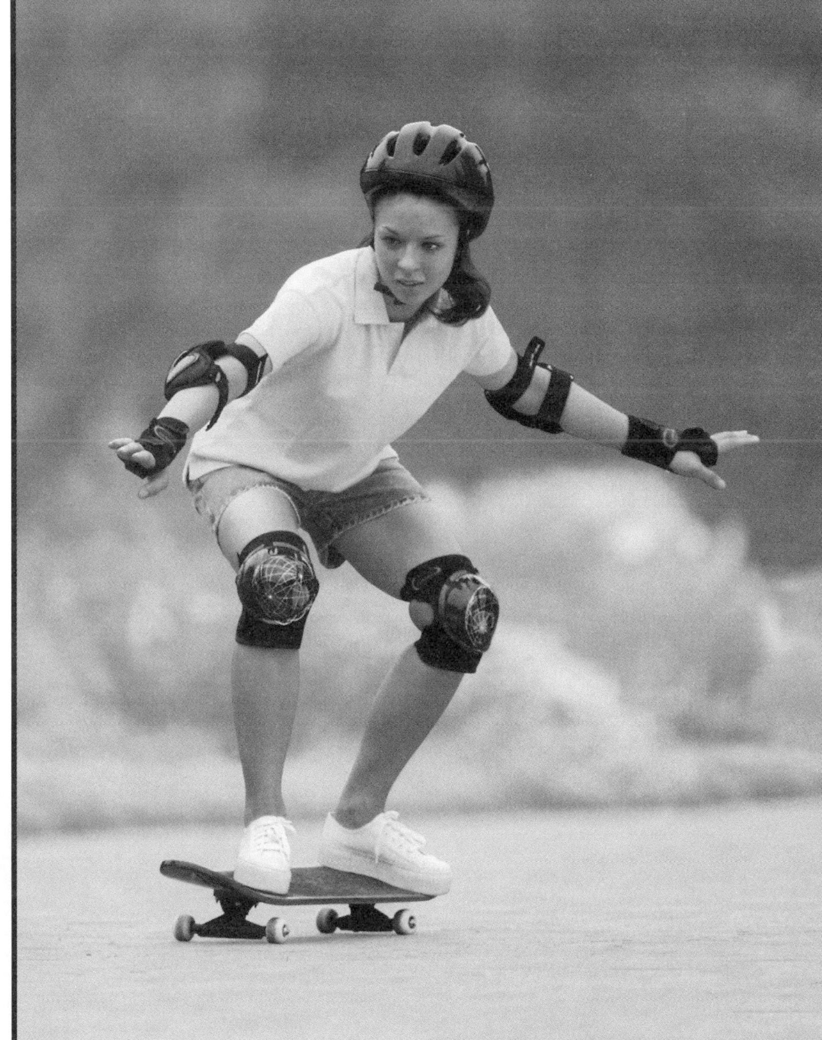

PHOTO CREDITS
Cover Photo: KS Studios

SRA/McGraw-Hill

A Division of The McGraw·Hill Companies

DECODING B1 MASTERY TEST 1
STUDENT PROFILE

Student _____________________   Teacher _____________________   Date _____________

	Skills tested		Number of errors	Pass criterion	Pass + Fail 0	If failed, review these lessons.
GROUP SECTION	**WORD IDENTIFICATION**					
	1	Writing Letters for Sounds		Pass if 0–1 error		27–30
	2	Writing Words without Endings		Pass if 0 errors		23, 25, 27, 29
	3	Matching Completion		Pass if 0 errors		1–4
	4	Sentence Copying		Pass if 0 errors		1–3
INDIVIDUAL SECTION	5	Short-Vowel Words		Pass if 0–1 error		1–9, 15, 16, 20, 25
	6	Long-Vowel Words		Pass if 0–1 error		6, 8–10, 24–26
	7	Sound Combinations		Pass if 0–1 error		1–9, 34, 35
	8	Word Endings *ed, ly, er*		Pass if 0–1 error		23, 26, 28–35
	9	Irregular Words		Pass if 0–1 error		27, 29–31
	STORY READING	**Time**				
	10	Rate (Time)			Pass if 80 secs. or less		28–35
	11	Accuracy (Errors)			Pass if 0–4 errors		28–35
	12	Comprehension		Pass if 0–1 error		28–35

TEST 1

1

___________ ___________ ___________ ___________ ___________

___________ ___________ ___________ ___________ ___________

2 The words in the first column have endings.
Write the same words without endings in the second column.

raked

dropping

nearly

shortest

grinned

3 Match the words and complete them.

beaten   fe

trash   ing

road   en

sleeping   sh

felt   r

4 Copy this sentence:
The tramp gets in shape.

____

Individual Section

5 pack   fell   ramp   win   dug

    not   get   bum   pit   drop

5 Errors _______

6 gate   hope   time   week   rider

    nose   fake   wheel   like   shape

6 Errors _______

7 holds   meal   sore   ranch   load

    reach   horse   board   coldest   heaps

7 Errors _______

8 sweeping   hammer   yearly   grinned   likely

    stayed   mopping   handed   popper   bigger

8 Errors _______

9 minutes   any   people   couldn't   money

9 Errors _______

10

The tramp was getting in shape. When he got up, the sun was coming up over the hill in the east. When he went to bed, the sun was dropping in the west. He worked and worked every day. He sheared sheep. He made gates and pens for pigs. He dug holes for trees. He was getting thinner and thinner.

The tramp had stayed at the ranch for ten weeks. He told the rancher, "I need more meat and beans." "Yes," she said. "You have worked and worked. You are faster and thinner. You may have more meat and beans.

10 Time ____________   **11** Errors ______

12

Record student's answers here:

1. When did the tramp go to bed?

____

2. Name 2 things the tramp did for work at the ranch.

____

3. How long did the tramp stay at the ranch?

____

4. What did the tramp tell the rancher he needed?

____

5. Did the tramp get more to eat?

____

12 Errors ______

Student _________________________   **Teacher** _________________________   **Date** _____________

		Skills tested	Number of errors	Pass criterion	Pass + Fail 0	If failed, review these lessons.
GROUP SECTION		**WORD IDENTIFICATION**				
	1	Identifying Letter Combinations		Pass if 0–1 error		40, 44, 45
	2	Writing Words without Endings		Pass if 0–1 error		52, 58–60
	3	Following Instructions		Pass if 0 errors		46, 47, 56
INDIVIDUAL SECTION	**4**	Writing Compound Words		Pass if 0 errors		37–40, 42–45, 48, 62
	5	Short-Vowel Words		Pass if 0–1 error		49, 51–53, 59
	6	Consonant Digraphs		Pass if 0–1 error		9, 12, 47, 48, 52
	7	*ed* Endings in Short-Vowel Words		Pass if 0–1 error		13, 49, 58–61
	8	Word Endings *s, ing, est, er,* and *ery*		Pass if 0–1 error		27, 31, 45, 49, 63, 64
	9	Sound Combinations *ai, oa, or, ol, ea, ou, ow*		Pass if 0–2 errors		51, 52, 55, 61, 62
	10	Irregular Words		Pass if 0–1 error		50, 57–63
		STORY READING — Time				
	11	Rate (Time)		Pass if 80 secs. or less		61–65
	12	Accuracy (Errors)		Pass if 0–4 errors		61–65
	13	Comprehension		Pass if 0–1 error		61–65

TEST 2

 **1** Cross out the words that don't have **wh.**

where	with	that	when	how	wheel
word	then	what	why	week	who

 **2** The words in the first column have endings.
Write the same words without endings in the second column.

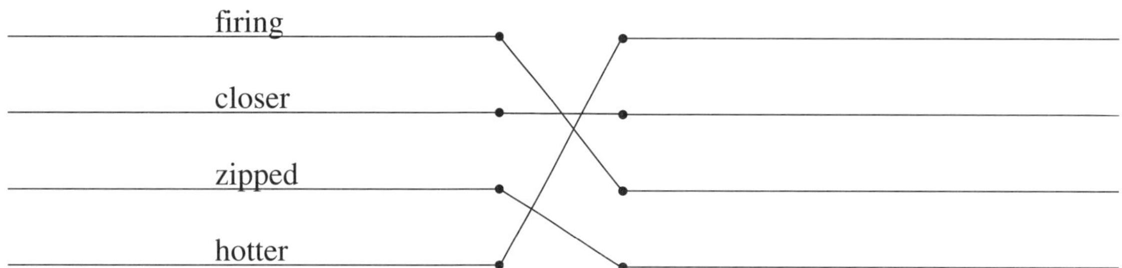

firing

closer

zipped

hotter

 **3** Write the word **louder.** Make a line over **loud.** _______________________

Write the word **first.** Make a line under **ir.** _______________________

4 Write the words.

may	+	be	=	
any	+	body	=	
near	+	ly	=	
her	+	self	=	

Individual Section

5

| plop | list | gum | dress | tramp |
| stand | crest | pond | fix | must |

5 Errors ______

6

| smash | when | chips | shop | things |
| whisper | there | fresh | wheels | brush |

6 Errors ______

7

| dressed | pinned | spotted | happened | handed |
| dragged | lifted | zipped | stepped | slammed |

7 Errors ______

8

| trying | plants | bragging | feels | slaps |
| fastest | slippery | campers | slowest | teller |

8 Errors ______

9

main	please	boards	form	bolt
painted	beat	grow	older	croak
could	loud	should	mouth	ouch

9 Errors ______

11

People were going in a ship from one land to another. They were sailing the sea when a bolt came out of the ship. And the ship began to sink. Men, women, and dogs were in the water. People were swimming and shouting. But the people and dogs were not sinking. They were holding on to boards. They yelled and yelled. One man did not yell. He whispered. This is what that man said, "I can't swim."

The other people grabbed on to him and kept him from sinking. Then a boat came by. A few people dragged him to the boat. When everybody was in the boat, they went to shore. They went faster and faster. They were saved.

11 Time _____________   **12** Errors _______

13 *Record student's answers here:*

1. Why did the ship begin to sink?

____

2. Why did the people not sink?

____

3. What did the one man whisper? _______________________________________

4. How did the people help him?

____

5. Where did they go in the boat? _______________________________________

13 Errors _______

Decoding Strategies

**Mastery Test Booklet
Decoding B1**

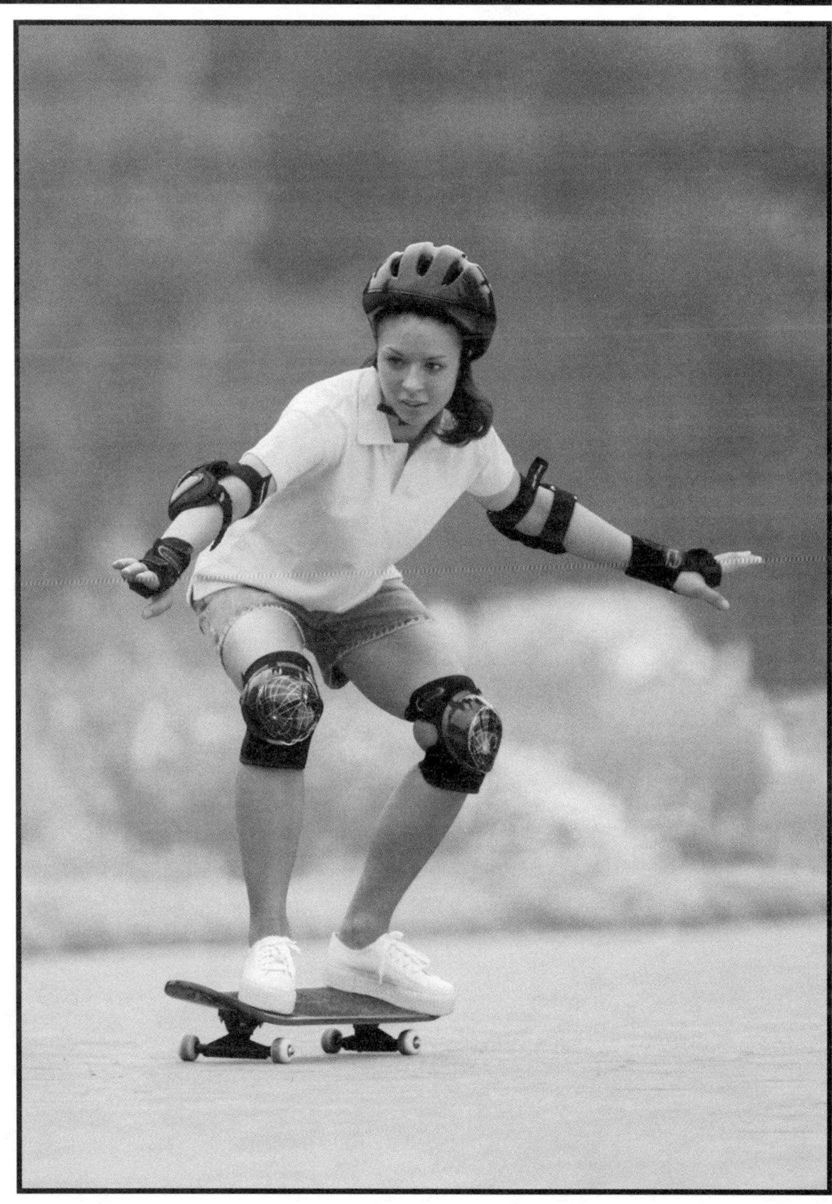

PHOTO CREDITS
Cover Photo: KS Studios

SRA/McGraw-Hill

A Division of The McGraw·Hill Companies

2002 Imprint
Copyright © 1999 by SRA/McGraw-Hill.

Send all inquiries to:
SRA/McGraw-Hill
8787 Orion Place
Columbus, Ohio 43240-4027

Printed in the United States of America.

R74782.01

13 14   MAZ 07 06 05 04

Student _________________________ **Teacher** _________________________ **Date** _____________

	Skills tested		Number of errors	Pass criterion	Pass + Fail 0	If failed, review these lessons.
GROUP SECTION	**WORD IDENTIFICATION**					
	1 Writing Letters for Sounds			Pass if 0–1 error		27–30
	2 Writing Words without Endings			Pass if 0 errors		23, 25, 27, 29
	3 Matching Completion			Pass if 0 errors		1–4
	4 Sentence Copying			Pass if 0 errors		1–3
INDIVIDUAL SECTION	**5** Short-Vowel Words			Pass if 0–1 error		1–9, 15, 16, 20, 25
	6 Long-Vowel Words			Pass if 0–1 error		6, 8–10, 24–26
	7 Sound Combinations			Pass if 0–1 error		1–9, 34, 35
	8 Word Endings *ed, ly, er*			Pass if 0–1 error		23, 26, 28–35
	9 Irregular Words			Pass if 0–1 error		27, 29–31
	STORY READING	**Time**				
	10 Rate (Time)			Pass if 80 secs. or less		28–35
	11 Accuracy (Errors)			Pass if 0–4 errors		28–35
	12 Comprehension			Pass if 0–1 error		28–35

TEST 1

NAME ___________________________________

1

___________ ___________ ___________ ___________

___________ ___________ ___________ ___________

2 The words in the first column have endings.
Write the same words without endings in the second column.

raked	
dropping	
nearly	
shortest	
grinned	

3 Match the words and complete them.

beaten	fe
trash	ing
road	en
sleeping	sh
felt	r

4 Copy this sentence:
The tramp gets in shape.

____

Individual Section

5   pack   fell   ramp   win   dug

    not   get   bum   pit   drop

5   Errors _______

6   gate   hope   time   week   rider

    nose   fake   wheel   like   shape

6   Errors _______

7   holds   meal   sore   ranch   load

    reach   horse   board   coldest   heaps

7   Errors _______

8   sweeping   hammer   yearly   grinned   likely

    stayed   mopping   handed   popper   bigger

8   Errors _______

9   minutes   any   people   couldn't   money

9   Errors _______

The tramp was getting in shape. When he got up, the sun was coming up over the hill in the east. When he went to bed, the sun was dropping in the west. He worked and worked every day. He sheared sheep. He made gates and pens for pigs. He dug holes for trees. He was getting thinner and thinner.

The tramp had stayed at the ranch for ten weeks. He told the rancher, "I need more meat and beans." "Yes," she said. "You have worked and worked. You are faster and thinner. You may have more meat and beans.

10 Time _______________   **11** Errors _______

12

Record student's answers here:

1. When did the tramp go to bed?

____

2. Name 2 things the tramp did for work at the ranch.

____

3. How long did the tramp stay at the ranch?

____

4. What did the tramp tell the rancher he needed?

____

5. Did the tramp get more to eat?

____

12 Errors _______

DECODING B1 MASTERY TEST 2
STUDENT PROFILE

Student _______________________ Teacher _______________________ Date _______________________

	Skills tested	Number of errors	Pass criterion	Pass + Fail 0	If failed, review these lessons.
GROUP SECTION	**WORD IDENTIFICATION**				
	1 Identifying Letter Combinations		Pass if 0–1 error		40, 44, 45
	2 Writing Words without Endings		Pass if 0–1 error		52, 58–60
	3 Following Instructions		Pass if 0 errors		46, 47, 56
INDIVIDUAL SECTION	**4** Writing Compound Words		Pass if 0 errors		37–40, 42–45, 48, 62
	5 Short-Vowel Words		Pass if 0–1 error		49, 51–53, 59
	6 Consonant Digraphs		Pass if 0–1 error		9, 12, 47, 48, 52
	7 *ed* Endings in Short-Vowel Words		Pass if 0–1 error		13, 49, 58–61
	8 Word Endings *s, ing, est, er,* and *ery*		Pass if 0–1 error		27, 31, 45, 49, 63, 64
	9 Sound Combinations *ai, oa, or, ol, ea, ou, ow*		Pass if 0–2 errors		51, 52, 55, 61, 62
	10 Irregular Words		Pass if 0–1 error		50, 57–63
	STORY READING — **Time**				
	11 Rate (Time)		Pass if 80 secs. or less		61–65
	12 Accuracy (Errors)		Pass if 0–4 errors		61–65
	13 Comprehension		Pass if 0–1 error		61–65

TEST 2

 **1** Cross out the words that don't have **wh.**

where	with	that	when	how	wheel
word	then	what	why	week	who

 **2** The words in the first column have endings.
Write the same words without endings in the second column.

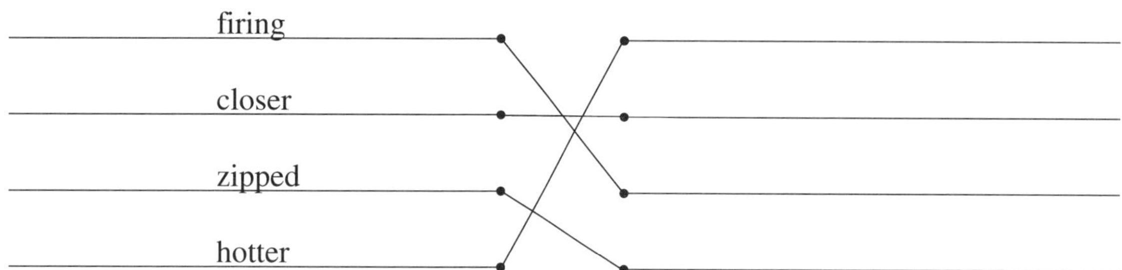

firing

closer

zipped

hotter

3 Write the word **louder.** Make a line over **loud.** _______________________

Write the word **first.** Make a line under **ir.** _______________________

 **4** Write the words.

may	+	be	=	
any	+	body	=	
near	+	ly	=	
her	+	self	=	

Individual Section

| **5** | plop | list | gum | dress | tramp | | **5** | Errors | ______ |
| | stand | crest | pond | fix | must | | | | |

| **6** | smash | when | chips | shop | things | | **6** | Errors | ______ |
| | whisper | there | fresh | wheels | brush | | | | |

| **7** | dressed | pinned | spotted | happened | handed | | **7** | Errors | ______ |
| | dragged | lifted | zipped | stepped | slammed | | | | |

| **8** | trying | plants | bragging | feels | slaps | | **8** | Errors | ______ |
| | fastest | slippery | campers | slowest | teller | | | | |

9	main	please	boards	form	bolt				
	painted	beat	grow	older	croak		**9**	Errors	______
	could	loud	should	mouth	ouch				

11

People were going in a ship from one land to another. They were sailing the sea when a bolt came out of the ship. And the ship began to sink. Men, women, and dogs were in the water. People were swimming and shouting. But the people and dogs were not sinking. They were holding on to boards. They yelled and yelled. One man did not yell. He whispered. This is what that man said, "I can't swim."

The other people grabbed on to him and kept him from sinking. Then a boat came by. A few people dragged him to the boat. When everybody was in the boat, they went to shore. They went faster and faster. They were saved.

11 Time _____________   **12** Errors _______

13 *Record student's answers here:*

1. Why did the ship begin to sink?

____

2. Why did the people not sink?

____

3. What did the one man whisper? _______________________________

4. How did the people help him?

____

5. Where did they go in the boat? _______________________________

13 Errors _______

Decoding Strategies

Mastery Test Booklet
Decoding B1

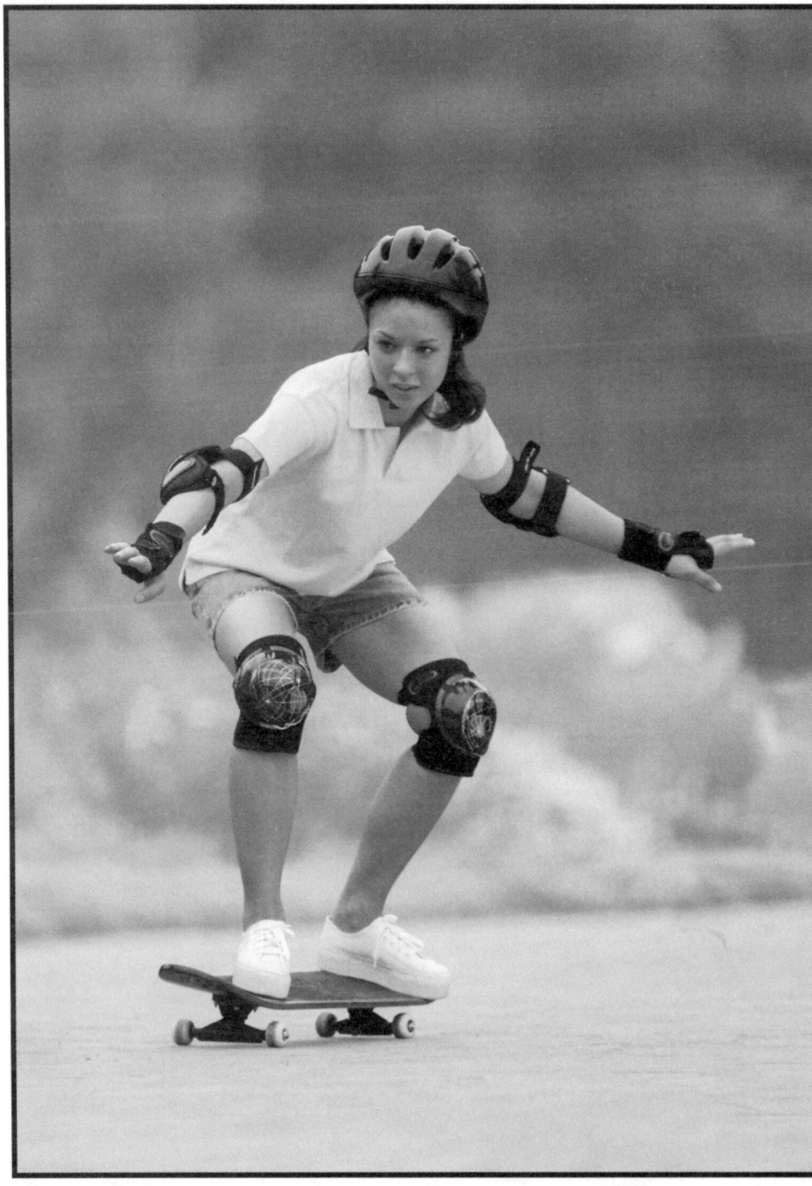

PHOTO CREDITS
Cover Photo: KS Studios

SRA/McGraw-Hill

A Division of The McGraw-Hill Companies

2002 Imprint
Copyright © 1999 by SRA/McGraw-Hill.

Send all inquiries to:
SRA/McGraw-Hill
8787 Orion Place
Columbus, Ohio 43240-4027

Printed in the United States of America.

R74782.01

13 14   MAZ 07 06 05 04

DECODING B1 MASTERY TEST 1
STUDENT PROFILE

Student ___________________   Teacher ___________________   Date ___________________

	Skills tested		Number of errors	Pass criterion	Pass + Fail 0	If failed, review these lessons.
GROUP SECTION	**WORD IDENTIFICATION**					
	1	Writing Letters for Sounds		Pass if 0–1 error		27–30
	2	Writing Words without Endings		Pass if 0 errors		23, 25, 27, 29
	3	Matching Completion		Pass if 0 errors		1–4
	4	Sentence Copying		Pass if 0 errors		1–3
INDIVIDUAL SECTION	5	Short-Vowel Words		Pass if 0–1 error		1–9, 15, 16, 20, 25
	6	Long-Vowel Words		Pass if 0–1 error		6, 8–10, 24–26
	7	Sound Combinations		Pass if 0–1 error		1–9, 34, 35
	8	Word Endings *ed, ly, er*		Pass if 0–1 error		23, 26, 28–35
	9	Irregular Words		Pass if 0–1 error		27, 29–31
	STORY READING	**Time**				
	10	Rate (Time)			Pass if 80 secs. or less		28–35
	11	Accuracy (Errors)			Pass if 0–4 errors		28–35
	12	Comprehension		Pass if 0–1 error		28–35

TEST 1

NAME _______________________

1

_______ _______ _______ _______ _______

_______ _______ _______ _______ _______

2 The words in the first column have endings.
Write the same words without endings in the second column.

raked

dropping

nearly

shortest

grinned

3 Match the words and complete them.

beaten	fe
trash	ing
road	en
sleeping	sh
felt	r

4 Copy this sentence:
The tramp gets in shape.

____

Individual Section

5 pack   fell   ramp   win   dug

not   get   bum   pit   drop

5 Errors _______

6 gate   hope   time   week   rider

nose   fake   wheel   like   shape

6 Errors _______

7 holds   meal   sore   ranch   load

reach   horse   board   coldest   heaps

7 Errors _______

8 sweeping   hammer   yearly   grinned   likely

stayed   mopping   handed   popper   bigger

8 Errors _______

9 minutes   any   people   couldn't   money

9 Errors _______

10

The tramp was getting in shape. When he got up, the sun was coming up over the hill in the east. When he went to bed, the sun was dropping in the west. He worked and worked every day. He sheared sheep. He made gates and pens for pigs. He dug holes for trees. He was getting thinner and thinner.

The tramp had stayed at the ranch for ten weeks. He told the rancher, "I need more meat and beans." "Yes," she said. "You have worked and worked. You are faster and thinner. You may have more meat and beans.

10 Time ______________   **11** Errors ______

12

Record student's answers here:

1. When did the tramp go to bed?

   ____

2. Name 2 things the tramp did for work at the ranch.

   ____

3. How long did the tramp stay at the ranch?

   ____

4. What did the tramp tell the rancher he needed?

   ____

5. Did the tramp get more to eat?

   ____

12 Errors ______

Student _________________________ **Teacher** _________________________ **Date** _____________

	Skills tested		Number of errors	Pass criterion	Pass + Fail 0	If failed, review these lessons.
GROUP SECTION	**WORD IDENTIFICATION**					
	1	Identifying Letter Combinations		Pass if 0–1 error		40, 44, 45
	2	Writing Words without Endings		Pass if 0–1 error		52, 58–60
	3	Following Instructions		Pass if 0 errors		46, 47, 56
INDIVIDUAL SECTION	**4**	Writing Compound Words		Pass if 0 errors		37–40, 42–45, 48, 62
	5	Short-Vowel Words		Pass if 0–1 error		49, 51–53, 59
	6	Consonant Digraphs		Pass if 0–1 error		9, 12, 47, 48, 52
	7	*ed* Endings in Short-Vowel Words		Pass if 0–1 error		13, 49, 58–61
	8	Word Endings *s, ing, est, er,* and *ery*		Pass if 0–1 error		27, 31, 45, 49, 63, 64
	9	Sound Combinations *ai, oa, or, ol, ea, ou, ow*		Pass if 0–2 errors		51, 52, 55, 61, 62
	10	Irregular Words		Pass if 0–1 error		50, 57–63
	STORY READING	**Time**				
	11	Rate (Time)		Pass if 80 secs. or less		61–65
	12	Accuracy (Errors)		Pass if 0–4 errors		61–65
	13	Comprehension		Pass if 0–1 error		61–65

TEST 2

 Cross out the words that don't have **wh.**

where   with   that   when   how   wheel

word   then   what   why   week   who

 The words in the first column have endings.
Write the same words without endings in the second column.

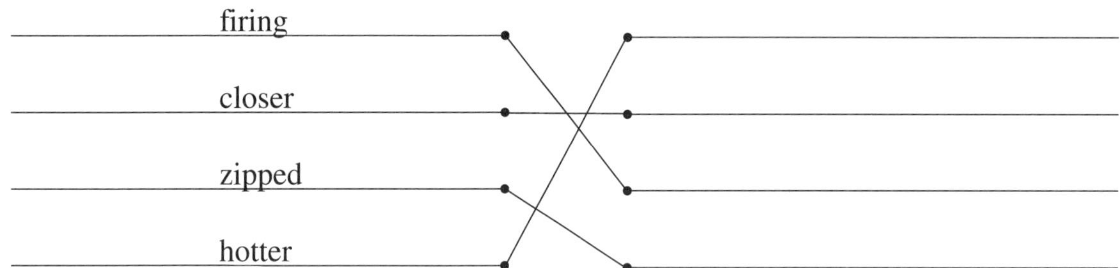

firing

closer

zipped

hotter

Write the word **louder.** Make a line over **loud.** _______________________

Write the word **first.** Make a line under **ir.** _______________________

Write the words.

may   +   be   =   _______________

any   +   body   =   _______________

near   +   ly   =   _______________

her   +   self   =   _______________

Individual Section

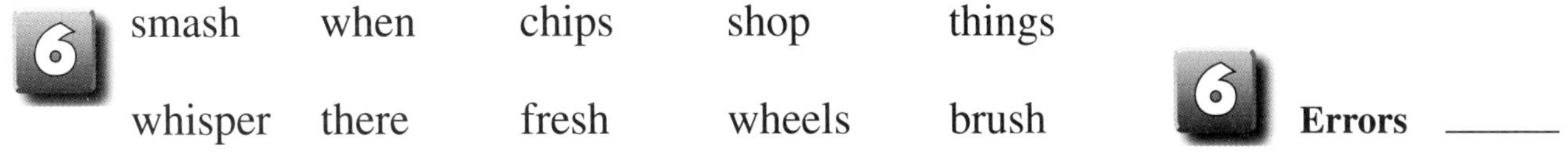

5 plop list gum dress tramp

stand crest pond fix must

5 Errors ______

6 smash when chips shop things

whisper there fresh wheels brush

6 Errors ______

7 dressed pinned spotted happened handed

dragged lifted zipped stepped slammed

7 Errors ______

8 trying plants bragging feels slaps

fastest slippery campers slowest teller

8 Errors ______

9 main please boards form bolt

painted beat grow older croak

could loud should mouth ouch

9 Errors ______

together   because   private   difference   done

what   millions   brother   know   who

10 Errors ______

11

People were going in a ship from one land to another. They were sailing the sea when a bolt came out of the ship. And the ship began to sink. Men, women, and dogs were in the water. People were swimming and shouting. But the people and dogs were not sinking. They were holding on to boards. They yelled and yelled. One man did not yell. He whispered. This is what that man said, "I can't swim."

The other people grabbed on to him and kept him from sinking. Then a boat came by. A few people dragged him to the boat. When everybody was in the boat, they went to shore. They went faster and faster. They were saved.

11 Time ______   **12** Errors ______

13 *Record student's answers here:*

1. Why did the ship begin to sink?

    ____

2. Why did the people not sink?

    ____

3. What did the one man whisper? ____

4. How did the people help him?

    ____

5. Where did they go in the boat? ____

13 Errors ______